ULTIMATE SURVIVORS

ULTIMATE SURVIVORS

Overcoming Life's Greatest Challenges

BOB GUTHRIE

CREATION
HOUSE

ULTIMATE SURVIVORS by Bob Guthrie
Published by Creation House
A Charisma Media Company
600 Rinehart Road
Lake Mary, Florida 32746
www.charismamedia.com

Unless otherwise noted, all Scripture quotations are from the New King James Version of the Bible. Copyright © 1979, 1980, 1982 by Thomas Nelson, Inc., publishers. Used by permission.

English definitions are from Webster's Dictionary.

Greek definitions are derived from *Strong's Exhaustive Concordance of the Bible*, ed. James Strong, Nashville, TN: Thomas Nelson Publishers, 1997.

Design Director: Bill Johnson
Cover design by Terry Clifton

Visit the author's website: www.ultimate-survivors.com

Library of Congress Cataloging-in-Publication Data:
2012918815
International Standard Book Number: 978-1-62136-317-0
E-book International Standard Book Number:
978-1-62136-318-7

First edition

12 13 14 15 16 — 9 8 7 6 5 4 3 2 1
Printed in the United States of America

DEDICATION

To Helen, whose input was indispensable in writing this book, and to our children: Scott, Lisa, Lori, Dan, and all their children. I hope that they, especially, will be encouraged by it. However, my intention is that all who would follow Jesus will be encouraged to hold fast His undeniable truths. These are what will abundantly sustain us in our seeking to be all that God has called us to be—even when things are most challenging.

ACKNOWLEDGMENTS

THIS BOOK WOULD never have happened had it not been for some very special people. Actually, they have touched the lives of all of us, at least in some small way, because they are largely responsible for what makes the body of Christ so precious.

You will find many of them scattered here and there amongst our well known preachers and teachers, to whom we all owe so much. But, they often show up in the least likely places because what sets these special ones apart is not that they are so well known. Rather, it is something so simple and low key that it's very easy to miss altogether. What makes them special is the love of Christ that we see in their readiness to receive us and welcome us into their presence.

They are so wonderfully approachable, and you find there's a certain warmth about them that assures you, you don't need to be something or do something to earn their acceptance. Their concern for our well being is obviously stronger than their need to impress us with their knowledge, or their importance. So when we leave them, we're feeling valued, appreciated, and now more able to handle the challenges before us.

Pastor Tom, mentioned herein, was a good example of these. It is my hope that this book will be a proper acknowledgment of their priceless service and will inspire many others to be one of them.

CONTENTS

INTRODUCTION

A couple of compelling concerns prompted the writing of this book—how to handle life's greatest hardships with joy, and how to overcome temptations that keep us from the best in life.

I was a hospital chaplain helping people deal with difficult medical challenges, and observing how God works for our benefit in the midst of our illnesses. It was at this time that we were startled by the news of two well-known Christian leaders having fallen into sexual immorality. We were deeply grieved with their failures. How could this happen to such godly leaders, and how can we avoid this ever happening again?

Over the next few years, I searched the scriptures for answers to these questions. God's Word reveals not only detailed insights to the root causes of our weaknesses and failures; but most importantly, He provides a path for both the cure and prevention that changes us from the core of our being outward. That's the good news! In this way we are best prepared for all of life's challenges; whether they are medical or financial tragedies, natural disasters, or persecutions; or whether they are personal tests of loneliness, addictions, or heartbreaking relationships.

And yet, there is something even more important than just enduring the trials of life—it's having the joy and fulfillment of ultimate surviving!

Chapter 1

THE CHALLENGE

Ultimate: Maximum, Farthest, Utmost

In response to the love of Christ, Ultimate Survivors hold in their heart the ultimate goal—to be all that God has called them to be. They believe that God loves them and has the best plan for their life, so they welcome His shaping and molding for the restoring of their soul. This enables them, not only to survive life's greatest trials, but to live with optimum joy and fulfillment.

Actually, all genuine spiritual growth comes from the process of our soul's being restored, which is the inevitable result of following the teachings of Jesus. Nevertheless, for many of us, the process often goes on without our being aware of why or how it is working in our life. This book investigates this vital aspect of our Christian walk. Our study uncovers clear, crisp perspectives on the key teachings of Jesus—like salvation, the soul, and faith—things which are too often muddied or blunted by the modern traditions of men. This gives us fuller understanding of His ways and allows us to know Him in a closer, deeper relationship.

The end result: we are better prepared to face the unprecedented difficulties of this present age by seeing the restoring of our soul more effectively applied in our everyday life, and thereby experience more of the exceedingly great rewards.

Always Reacting

Our investigation begins at the very core of our being where every one of us is faced with a challenge. There in the deepest depths of our heart, whether we are conscious of it or not, you and I are always and unavoidably reacting in some way to The Challenge. And right along with us, every other living person is also reacting to The Challenge. This is true, regardless of social status, income, education, or religion.

On this earth we are always dealing with challenges, and all too often they seem to come in bundles. However, this challenge is absolutely the most demanding and most risky, and yet it's the most rewarding. It is ongoing and underlies all of our other challenges. The way we are responding to it determines how well we handle, or survive, all the others. In fact, the way we interact with The Challenge has more to do with the entire shaping of our life than all other things put together.

If these strong statements are true, why The Challenge and where does it come from?

From the time we are born into this world and throughout our lifetime, every human being is continually confronted with three basic realities of life. Just as with The Challenge, we may be unaware of these realities and the enormous impact they can have on our life. Nevertheless, out of all of life's realities, these three have the awesome potential for making our life either utterly empty and desperately dis-appointing or joyful and wonderfully fulfilling, depending on how we deal with them. For this reason, God, in His loving-kindness, sets The Challenge before us because it is the way to successfully deal with these three nonnegotiable realities.

There are oodles of programs that are being promoted as a way of dealing with life's problems. The world's culture goes to great lengths to make ineffective programs appear very attractive and easy to follow. Because God is love, He gives us freedom to make our own choice in this. In spite of The Challenge's great promises, deciding whether or not to accept it is not easy. Like any challenge worthy of being called a challenge, it offers both rewards and risks. But this one, along with the risks, offers the greatest rewards!

Ultimate Survivors are those who have accepted and are fully engaged in The Challenge. The intention of this book is to serve up for each reader a tantalizing taste of the rewards so they also will desire to be an Ultimate Survivor and accept The Challenge.

The best understanding of The Challenge and what it means to survive is found in the major biblical themes and especially in the teachings of Jesus where it is presented loud and clear. And yet, tragically, it is widely misunderstood or just overlooked, even by many longtime Christians. Then, when it does come to the attention of the faint at heart, it may simply be ignored because at first encounter the personal costs may appear so scary that they deceptively hide the unspeakable rewards.

Whether or not a person answers The Challenge, the remarkable truth is that anyone can profit substantially from the insights that can be gained from just having a better understanding of the three realities that prompted it. So let's have a look at these realities and learn more about The Challenge. Survival in any situation requires a realistic understanding of the existing factors that might be either working for or against our surviving.

REALITY 1: CREATED IN GOD'S IMAGE

On a regular basis for about a year, I used to receive in the mail a gospel tract, skillfully disguised as a credit card offer by one of our country's largest banks. I would always see this phrase placed boldly, right there under its logo: "The Right Relationship is Everything." I thought, *Now these guys are pretty clever! With only five words they have ingeniously placed the gospel message right there before my eyes—because "right relationship" is at the very heart of the gospel message.* And it is the central issue in The Challenge. But what does "right relationship" have to do with surviving life's worst trials? Let's see.

God said, "Let Us make man in Our image" (Gen. 1:26). One of the most important aspects of "our image" has to be their special relationship of closeness. It's that one supreme, perfect togetherness known as the three in one. It's the only existing model that shows how to be perfectly relating to others. Every facet of our being is either significantly helped or harmed, depending on whether or not we are in right relationship with God and others.

At the center of what we are, there is another reflection of God that is the most significant because it's the single motive for right relationship. *Love* is the one word that best describes God and all His motives and actions. This is why He, who created all things for His pleasure, created us for the primary purpose of being lovingly bonded together with Him, receiving and giving love.

God, who is love, is always working to make our bonding stronger and our fellowship more precious until, finally, somewhere in the heavens there is the marriage of all marriages. It's a great mystery, God becoming one with us, His creation. And yet, it's just what Jesus prayed for: "As You, Father, are in Me, and I in You; that they also may be one in Us" (John 17:21). Now that's ultimate closeness of the right kind!

An essential part of this closeness is to know and be known. To say you love someone is only significant to the depth that you know them. God has strong feelings about this. Isaiah, Jeremiah, Hosea, and Amos are some of God's powerful spokesmen in the Old Testament who wrote about God's fervent desire to be known. In speaking for God, Jeremiah said if someone wants to boast about anything, let him boast in the fact "that he understands and knows Me" (Jer. 9:24).

Ultimate Survivors are committed to growing in their understanding of the Lord and coming to know Him more fully. The alternative seems unthinkable; nevertheless, the most painful words anyone will ever have to hear will be spoken on that day when Jesus will say to some, "I never knew you; depart from Me" (Matt. 7:23).

Occasionally, while I was serving as a hospital chaplain, someone would ask me what church or denomination I was a part of. I believe they were usually concerned about doctrine. Because if they thought I could be a carrier of some "weird teaching," they might not want to let me get too close for fear that it might rub off on them.

So, I would reply, "When I was in the business world there was a popular saying which I found to be quite true: 'What brings success in business is not what you know, but who you know.' Now, I find that's also true in religion, so I'm pleased to say I know a very important person; His name is Jesus." With that, some might falter for a moment or two, but then they would usually say, "Yah, that's good." Things usually flowed quite nicely after that.

But how is it possible to know and be known by someone who is invisible to the natural eye? God made this possible by arranging for us to have the ultimate in fellowship when He created us with a spirit that enables us to actually experience His presence and even be one with Him. "But he who is joined to the Lord is one spirit with Him" (1 Cor. 6:17).

Remember, He's the one who chose and arranged for this by creating us in His image. Consequently, being stamped with the image of God imparts our deepest and strongest motivating desire because that's His desire. Namely, it is to be in this close relationship with Him, giving and receiving love.

Because of His loving nature, God gives us total freedom of choice. He never compels us in any way to participate in this warmest of friendships. He's the most amazing person, very thoughtful of others and a perfect gentleman. He doesn't even force the fact of His existence upon us, which it seems He has every right to do—but that's not what He does.

He gives us just enough clear evidence so we can find Him if we really want to. But He doesn't give us too much undeniable evidence so if we really don't want to find Him, we are not compelled to. Love isn't love if it is forced.

However, we have absolutely no choice in this matter of our design. God, as the Creator, had freedom to create all things just as it pleased Him—and this is what pleased Him. So there's no way to deny this dominant need of love. It would be like trying to outrun your own shadow; you'll never be able to separate yourself from this basic aspect of what you are. It makes no difference if you're the richest person in the world, a beggar, a rocket scientist, or a prostitute—to be loved and appreciated is the primary motive in your life.

Strategies of using money, power, or sex are commonly used with the hope of obtaining true love or to avoid losing it. A hermit's lifestyle is usually an attempt to avoid the pain of being rejected for the thing he most desires. Yet the most deeply satisfying experiences can be found in this love connection with God. That's why those special, most meaningful times we have with others take place when we are sharing this relationship.

It's the place where we will always have the opportunity for optimum fulfillment because it's where our basic, most essential needs are met—like a sense of purpose, a feeling that we belong, and the assurance that we're valued and sincerely appreciated. When this place, for which we were created, is wholeheartedly accepted and lived in, it is totally satisfying as nothing else can be. David said it this way: "Because Your loving kindness is better than life, my lips shall praise You" (Ps. 63:3).

This special connection is unique; it's the place where genuine love is found. Those in the world, apart from God, are limited in their ability to love. Real love can't be found or worked up through our own efforts apart from God because love originates in Him. "Everyone who loves is born of God and knows God" (1 John 4:7). On the other hand, "He who does not love does not know God, for God is love" (v. 8). For all of these reasons, I call this most special relationship "The Love Connection," or "TLC."

There is no better preparation for handling life's troubles than to have the security that's found exclusively in TLC, a rock solid foundation for our life. So, The Challenge is an invitation to embark on a lifelong quest with this first objective: find The Love Connection!

REALITY 2: INHERITED INDEPENDENT NATURE

The Love Connection can bring such love, joy, and peace to a person's life; so why are there some people who are not interested in knowing God, the One who is TLC? And what about those who have known Him for a while but seem not at all interested in knowing Him any better? Or, what about us; have there been times in our life when we have turned our back on Him?

It only happened three or four times when I was very young, and each time was a special moment. My mother would say to me, "Bobbie, when Momma was carrying you in her tummy, I pleaded with God to give me a son. Finally, I said to God, 'You give me a son and I will dedicate him to You.'"

My parents were always actively involved church members; however, mother had a special relationship with God. She died because of complications at my birth, and then, after a short time, came back to life. Out of body experiences were pooh-poohed in those days. But she made a point of telling each of us five kids about the beauty, the wonder, and especially the peace that she had encountered somewhere above the clouds. She said she was climbing a hill covered with the most gorgeous flowers and had no desire to return, but Jesus appeared at the top of the hill and said, "Go on back now; I have more for you to do." Her emphatic words to me were, "I don't care what anybody says; that was the most real experience of my life."

I grew up with lots of encouragement to do what is right

and good. Shortly after receiving Jesus Christ as my Lord and Savior when I was in grade school, my sister and I were playing games one day on the floor. For no apparent reason, I stood up and said, "You know, Ruthie, I don't think God will ever let me rest until I become a minister." I sat back down and didn't give it another thought while we resumed playing as though nothing had happened. On up through high school I had a warm relationship with God, but in college I began to drift away from Him.

In my family and the church I grew up in, I don't remember hearing anything about how to deal with feeling "not quite good enough." For whatever the reason, I missed getting real solidly grounded in God's love for me "just as I am." Consequently, my ability to have satisfying relations with others was limited—I felt alone.

I went to college without any conscious awareness of my vulnerability, yet I wanted to feel included and appreciated. So I chose the path that is so easy for a young man in a college fraternity—I turned away from what was right to what I knew was wrong. I am extremely grateful that God showed me His loving-kindness and eventually restored me to an even more wonderful friendship, but it took some time because I was a slow learner.

Is there possibly some sort of a basic resistance to God that we all have known? A few years ago, researchers studying the DNA concluded there once existed a "Mitochondrial Eve" or "African Eve." The study strongly supports the notion that we all came from the same mother. Of course, the biblical record also shows how we all came from the same father, "Adam." Furthermore, the Bible shows how we inherited an independent nature from this same father.

What we've inherited from him is not money to be

deposited in our bank account. Instead, it is a spiritual DNA, which has been deposited in the depths of our soul where, unfortunately, it has a powerful negative effect on all our interactions with God and others. The Book of Proverbs puts it like this, "Foolishness is bound up in the heart of a child" (Prov. 22:15). Foolishness is a good name for our inherited nature because it stubbornly works against what is best for us and the others around us. Even though we're created with the God-given desires in our heart that long to be fulfilled in TLC, this inherited nature strongly resists that. And even as it is only a part of our soul, it strives to totally dominate our makeup to motivate and direct us in a vain attempt to live successfully apart from The Love Connection.

Even those who we would call "good Christians" can have a great deal of trouble with this inherited nature. How about the apostle Paul? Wouldn't we agree he was a pretty solid believer? It must be this same nature he was talking about that was giving him a real problem: "But I see another law in my members, warring against the law of my mind" (Rom. 7:23). This was happening when he was trying to do what's good. However, when it's the dominant nature oper-ating in us, it can be so deceptively subtle that we might not be consciously aware of it at all. However, this deception is always much easier to detect in others.

Depending on the progress God has already made in the restoring of our soul, this inherited nature can make a person very unpleasant to be around, or maybe so obnox-ious that others choose to avoid them all together. Then, unfortunately, we have seen those instances when it has erupted with such ugly violence that it shocks everyone who witnesses it. The news stories of someone going on a killing rampage are becoming more common because so many more people are living in this independent nature rather than in the loving nature God makes available for us. Nevertheless, at the same time that things are growing worse and worse around us, God is working more powerfully in restoring the souls of His children to live more successfully above the storms.

Just like we had no choice in the matter of our being created in God's image, we also had no choice in this matter of the nature we inherited. It certainly is not our fault that we were born that way. But the reality is we have a problem; it's there, deep in the center of our being from the moment of our birth. Would you say it could be a major hindrance in our dealing with the trials of life? So, what should we do about it?

Above all, be comforted with this truth: God is always working diligently in your life and mine for our very best interests. He's taking this mixed nature of ours along with all our circumstances and working them together for our good, as long as we love Him and go along with His plan. Furthermore, people often give up on people; but God *never* gives up on you. That's why Paul could say, "Being confident of this very thing, that He who has begun a good work in you will complete it until the day of Jesus Christ" (Phil. 1:6).

How it all came about

If we don't know the real roots and depth of a problem, how can we expect to have a total cure and the full satisfaction that is promised? So let's have a look at how this independent nature was formed and how it so powerfully influences our lives. Our best source of information is in the Book of Genesis. Here is a record of God's conversation with Adam after his sin of eating the forbidden fruit.

By observing Adam's actions we will see the unfolding of at least five key traits of this nature.

> So he said, "I heard Your voice in the garden, and I was afraid because I was naked; and I hid myself." And He said, "Who told you that you were naked? Have you eaten from the tree of which I commanded you that you should not eat?" Then the man said, "The woman whom You gave to be with me, she gave me of the tree, and I ate."
>
> —Genesis 3:10–12

First, we see Adam was "fearing." Then we see he was "lying" because his real reason for fearing was that he knew he had done what was wrong. Next, he was covering up and "hiding." When he said Eve was the one who gave him the fruit, he was "blaming" someone else for his sin. Most noteworthy is Adam's "Self-serving," which is apparent throughout the episode. Without any apparent hesitation, he put his own interests above any concern for God's or Eve's interests.

Self-serving

Notice how Adam's actions of fearing, lying, hiding, and blaming were preceded by a very important inward action, a pivotal decision in his heart. When someone loves God wholeheartedly, they are open to God's love and trust His plan for their life. In this case, however, Adam did what everyone else does when they disobey God; he hardened his heart against God's love. He ignored the One who had shown extraordinary compassion for him, and then he disgraced his wife without any sign of compassion. He was definitely putting his interests before anybody else's.

So, let's call this independent nature the "I-nature." It

expresses itself like this: "I have a better plan, and I'm looking out for me!"

Adam, as well as you and I, were created with the foremost desire to be loved and to love others. Consequently, our greatest fear is being found to be unlovable, unworthy of being included, rejected. Choosing to lean on his own understanding instead of trusting God's ways for satisfying these desires of his heart had left Adam alone and outside of The Love Connection.

But as a result of his actions, he became fearful. He had reason to feel alone after he had moved himself outside of the presence of God's love. Also, after sinning he most likely felt he "wasn't worthy" of being included. Whatever the case, he did nothing to correct the disposition of his heart. He could have admitted his sin and experienced a quick restoration of fellowship with God.

This is why there's a universal notion all of us are born with. When we are aware of it, it may be sort of a faint, uneasy feeling hiding somewhere inside of us. Occasionally it prompts a fleeting thought, like, "I feel I'm just not good enough in some way." Honestly facing such feelings takes some humility; our attempts to squelch them often masquerade as pride.

Now, remember, we didn't do something wrong because we were born with these traits. Nevertheless, by their very nature they are always energizing our efforts to hide the fact of their presence, especially when we are trying to look "good." They are also right on hand to help quickly justify any of our shortcomings that might have been uncovered. They rate right up there with the greatest conspiracies, working so skillfully under cover that they can effectively hide their presence even from ourselves. This is why it's true, "Every way of a man is right in his own eyes" (Prov. 21:2).

Innocent babies

So, it's understandable that while these traits are hard to detect in ourself, they are quite easy to detect in others. Yes, even in "pure and innocent" babies we will see excellent demonstrations of this I-nature once they are old enough to get around a bit and haven't become too polished in their social interactions. Observant parents soon recognize the evidence of their child's Self-serving, looking out for number one. Without any qualms, he might yank a toy away from another kid, hurting him in the process and leave him crying, but show no remorse.

He is amazingly well self-taught when it comes to putting the blame somewhere else for wrongs he has done. And no one needs to teach him how to lie or how to cover up some forbidden act. It's also very apparent he wants to run the show. Even though he's pretty new on the scene, just like Adam was, he's sure he knows better than anyone else what's best for him. Perhaps we all have gotten a kick out of these "home videos," but here's the not-so-humorous side. This I-nature directly opposes our being in The Love Connection. Unless it is dealt with, it creates two devastating results:

First, it deprives us of our greatest joy because fearing, lying, hiding, and blaming isolate us from love relationship with God and others. We can't have meaningful relationships with others, giving and receiving love, when we're too afraid that being close might reveal "something's wrong" with us.

Secondly, not having any close relationships at all can leave us feeling utterly alone. Billy Graham said in one of his crusades that loneliness was our greatest problem. When I've asked alcoholics why they drink, the most frequent response was, "To ease the pain." When I questioned them further about the pain, eventually we would uncover the fact that they didn't have the kind of closeness in their personal relations with God and others where they could experience genuine love and feel securely accepted.

The world knows our pain and seductively offers us fake love relationships, like illicit sexual relations and pornography. But then it also offers drugs, alcohol, overeating, and hundreds of various addictions that can only give temporary relief or momentary distraction from the pain. We have to deal with the pain of loneliness because this is when we're so vulnerable to the destructive temptations of the world. It's very difficult surviving life's trials and temptations when we're separated from TLC, which is the most secure and satisfying foundation for our life. We don't survive or do anything worthwhile apart from God. "For without Me you can do nothing" (John 15:5).

Here we are with this I-nature and its own built-in, highly effective program for making it look like it's a very "natural" and "OK" part of us. But actually it has two terrible potentials. It can deprive us of our greatest joy, and it can cause us our greatest pain. The good news is that God has a plan that can totally solve our problem and set us free. So our quest continues.

The Challenge is an invitation to embark on a lifelong quest with these first two objectives—to find and protect The Love Connection!

Reality 3: Born in a Cosmic Conflict

We are born into a raging conflict so intense and enormous in scope that it involves every person and creature in the entire universe. The conflict is a contest between two kingdoms, each with an unwavering objective that places them in fierce opposition where there is no possibility of compromise, only winning or losing.

One of these kingdoms is ruled by Jesus, the Son of God, who has proven by His words and actions that He is what He says He is—"the way, the truth, and the life" (John 14:6). The other kingdom is ruled by Satan, who has proven by his words and actions that he is what Jesus said of him—"a liar and the father of it" (John 8:44). Jesus made a factual assessment of the conflict and revealed the strategies of both kingdoms.

> He who is not with Me is against Me, and he who does not gather with Me scatters abroad.
> —Matthew 12:30

> The thief does not come except to steal, and to kill, and to destroy. I have come that they may have life, and that they may have it more abundantly.
> —John 10:10

This is why every person is on one side of the struggle or the other; there is no neutral position nor is there any chance for just sitting it out on the sidelines. This is why, whether we are aware or not, each one of us is in some way either gathering with Jesus or helping the devil to scatter.

With his lies and deceptions, the devil's scheme is to divert us from ever dealing with the root cause of our problems—our separation from TLC. Using his easier access through our I-nature, he is working to deceive us so that we are always driven in a fruitless effort, trying to cope with only the symptoms of our problems. This keeps us vulnerable to his devices because it sidetracks us from a satisfying relationship with Jesus and the genuine joy and peace that He has for us.

We are exceedingly fortunate that Jesus—the Christ, anointed by God to rule—is always drawing us into a closer walk with Him. He wants us to have His joy: the kind that isn't just pasted on the outside of us but the kind that is like the Holy Spirit springing up from our innermost being. For this reason, those who accept The Challenge will see that God's plan deals with the root of problems, restoring us from the core of our being outward for the true satisfaction that is found in meaningful relationship with Him and being rightly related to others.

Here's the most exciting good news. The Holy Bible, which is the only proven predictor of the future, shows how our submitting to Jesus Christ's authority restores us by a process that at the same time prepares His kingdom to be the everlasting kingdom that will replace all other kingdoms. This worldwide, earthshaking development is being closely followed with eager anticipation throughout the breadth of the whole universe. Yet God is bringing it together with His focus on you and me and on whosoever will in order that we may be gatherers, our souls may be restored, and we may have the fullness of joy that Jesus offers us.

The Challenge follows God's plan, which equips us very well for life's most difficult trials, but it is always pointing beyond that and is leading us to ultimate surviving—fulfilling God's highest calling for our life. So, The Challenge is an invitation to embark on a lifelong quest to find, protect, and complete The Love Connection.

Now, on to The Challenge!

.

Chapter 2

FINDING THE LOVE
CONNECTION

Tom Jackson

When I met Tom Jackson, I was a young stock-broker struggling to look every bit the part of a successful businessman. But my biggest problem was a basic insecurity, which I was not able to admit to anyone, especially to myself. I was instantly defensive and self-justifying, and I always had to be on guard with people who showed interest in me because I "just knew" they couldn't be interested in me just for me.

Tom was a pastor who I quickly grew to appreciate because he seemed genuine. He was manly, the kind of guy I could respect. In spite of my obnoxious character, he had the God-given ability to accept me as I was. For that reason, his impact on my life was enormous. In one of Tom's personal growth groups, I began letting others get to know me. I found there was forgiveness for my failures and acceptance of my shortcomings. Because of God's love and acceptance shown to me by Tom and those in the group, significant changes began taking place in my life. I was restored to a closer relationship with God than when I accepted Christ as a young boy.

I knew God's love was changing me because my fears were fading. One incident with Tom is fun to share and it illustrates the point. At one of my counseling sessions with him, he said he was going to recommend me for the long-range planning committee of the church. The fact that he would even think of recommending me for such a prestigious committee after he had come to know me so well just blew me away. The people on that committee were very highly regarded, like one fine gentleman who a little later became president of one of our nation's strongest banks.

The recent changes in my life plus this special gesture of love sent me home floating on a cloud. But approaching the large, mansion-like house on that dark, stormy day was like walking into a scary movie. Several of us bachelors were renting this stately home from the owner who was a high-level consultant back in Washington, D.C.

After driving into the huge, underground garage, I went up to the main floor. Rather than continuing on up a narrow, hidden stairway to my quarters, I wandered into the living room. It appeared I was alone, but I could never be sure in that old house. There were always unusual noises, especially on that day, like the shutters banging and creaking and the toilet upstairs somewhere that every so often seemed to be flushing all on its own.

I glanced into the den with its walls of books and its heavy, black leather furniture and the suit of knight's armor standing there; but there was no one there. I sprawled out on the rug with the TV on. I was not really watching, only basking in a warm, secure feeling of having some value as a person and being sincerely appreciated. I got up, wandered into the kitchen, and looked out into the dark, wooded thicket close to the house. A childhood thought popped into my mind: *What if a big, mean boogeyman were to crash through that door right now?* I was a little surprised but actually pleased with my response that came without hesitation: "Come on in, have a cup of coffee and relax a bit." The awesome power of love was changing me.

A HEALTHY UNCOMFORTABLE

As long as we're reasonably comfortable with the way things appear to be going, there's a tendency to believe we're OK and we don't need to consider making any changes.

However, sometimes our greatest opportunities for worthwhile, spiritual growth are the result of our having become very uncomfortable. Is there a "good uncomfortable?" How does someone come to the point of feeling that they need TLC? Jesus has explained how a "healthy uncomfortable" can lead to incredible blessings.

> Blessed are the poor in spirit, For theirs is the kingdom of heaven.
>
> Blessed are those who mourn, For they shall be comforted.
>
> Blessed are the meek, For they shall inherit the earth.
>
> Blessed are those who hunger and thirst for righteousness, For they shall be filled.
> —MATTHEW 5:3–6

We are in an excellent place to be blessed when we are poor in spirit. That's when we are recognizing that something important must be missing in our life, we may be lacking joy and satisfaction, or we don't seem to have what we need to face our challenges. That's when we're more open to the good things God has for us in His kingdom.

When this "poor" feeling is uncomfortable enough and we're not just stuffing it away somewhere but are able to admit our grief, it can be the motivation that turns us to Him so we can get pointed in the direction that leads to being truly comforted. Then, if we're meek enough to submit to Him and trust Him, He will work amazing things in our life because that's being the kind of person He likes to exalt.

> For the eyes of the LORD run to and fro throughout the whole earth, to show Himself strong on behalf of those whose heart is loyal to Him.
> —2 CHRONICLES 16:9

> Therefore humble yourselves under the mighty hand of God, that He may exalt you in due time.
> —1 PETER 5:6

Too often we seem to find ourself struggling to solve our discomfort by foolishly pursuing dead-end solutions, which we eventually find can never satisfy. What fully satisfies comes from hungering and thirsting for righteousness— that's having a right relationship with God. And when we find that, we find TLC.

FEAR OF GOD

In seeking to be rightly related with God, it's important to recognize how one of our heart's most powerful functions can either detour us or greatly motivate us in diligently seeking Him. We're talking about fear. Understanding fear is essential in our search for TLC. It's an obvious place to begin our search because of the major role it played in Adam and Eve's sinning, and in the forming of our I-nature. The "book of wisdom" gives us an excellent starting point: "The fear of the LORD is the beginning of wisdom" (Prov. 9:10).

But some will say we don't need to "fear" God; we just need to "reverence" Him. Reverencing God is indispensable, and I'm sure we need to reverence Him more; but our deeper need is to fear Him. Let me explain. For most of us, especially until we are born again, actually don't fear Him enough. There are a couple of ways we might look at the idea of "fearing God."

The first way is to fear Him in thinking that He's just sitting up there, ready to make some serious trouble for us if we don't behave. After all, He's the One, and the only One, who can destroy both our body and soul in hell (see Matthew 10:28).

A number of years ago a great comedian, Jonathan Winters, was playing the part of a little old lady setting on her front porch. When a reporter taking a political poll asked him what he wanted in a president, Jonathan answered, "I want him to be a God fear'n man." The reporter asked, "Oh, you want him to be religious?" Jonathan quickly responded, "Oh no! I just want him to fear God so if he goofs, God'll get'im."

We don't have to be "religious" to have the fear that God might "get us." As a matter of fact, until things are thoroughly worked out with God, anyone can have some lingering awareness of deserving to be punished for something, while not consciously knowing what the "something" is. The good news is that Jesus shows us how to handle both the weakest and the strongest fears because He came to "release those who through fear of death were all their lifetime subject to bondage" (Heb. 2:15).

We are approaching the basic root of fear, when we ask

why Adam became fearful after he sinned. Isn't it that he knew in his heart he deserved punishment because he had disobeyed God? The Word tells us that fear has punishment (see 1 John 4:18; Matthew 25:46).

It's true the fear of a dangerous enemy who's threatening to kill us can be terrifying. But the other way of fearing God goes much deeper than fear of physical harm. Our deeper and stronger fear is that we might do something that would cause us to lose the approval of the person or persons whose love is most precious to us. So in this sense, we can love a lot of people; but the one we are most fearful of offending is the one we love most. It's a good thing to ask ourselves every so often, "Who am I most fearful of offending today?"

Our Father, who loves us dearly, is concerned about our deepest fear. "Fear of the LORD is the beginning of wisdom"; but here's another side of the coin: "The fear of man brings a snare" (Prov. 9:10; 29:25). We don't want people to be displeased with us. We want to have the approval of others and to be lovingly included—God created us with that desire. That's why it's so gratifying when we have the approval of those we love.

This spotlights one of our most common problems, the one that most strongly imprisons us. All too often we are more fearful of losing the approval of others than we are of losing God's approval. That traps us because no matter how hard we work at it, we are never "good enough" for man's approval.

PEELING THE ONION

Through Pastor Tom's acceptance and counsel, I had definitely become less fearful of losing man's approval. Then bigger gains came after getting married and heading off to seminary, which turned out to be a significant encounter with God that we'll have a good look at later. However, God deals with our fear of man in the same way He brings about change in most of the areas of our life—like peeling an onion one layer at a time. So, a couple of years after graduating from seminary, God was still peeling this onion of fear.

I was serving as a chaplain in Wenatchee, Washington, at the hospital where I was born—something I could never have even imagined beforehand. Remember, this was where my mother died and came back to tell about it. While I was there on staff, she died the second time. I wasn't deeply disturbed by her passing because I knew she would be climbing a hill that she had already been on once before, and I knew how to get to that same hill.

> Who may ascend into the hill of the LORD? Or who may stand in His holy place? He who has clean hands and a pure heart, who has not lifted up his soul to an idol, nor sworn deceitfully.
> —PSALM 24:3–4

Also, this is where my wife, Helen, gave birth to the last three of our four children. I sensed God was walking the halls with me, allowing me to bless patients in a special way on His behalf. There were four young doctors, outstanding both for their medical excellence and their commitment to God, who solidly backed me in my ministry at the hospital.

One day I said something very stupid in their presence. After leaving them, I was harshly rebuking myself for being so obnoxious. These guys were such a blessing, and now I had probably lost their respect forever. After arriving at my office, I continued whining about the problem when it suddenly occurred to me I was more fearful of losing their approval than I was of losing God's. From the depths of my heart, I asked Him for forgiveness. I gave those guys to God, reminding Him and myself that He was far more precious to me. I accepted His forgiveness, left the matter behind, and went on with my day.

The next time I saw them, amazingly, everything was quite normal. It was as though my goof had never happened, and they have not mentioned it since. It's true that God had peeled off a few layers before this incident and many since; but this one made a remarkable change in my life.

I was surprised by the new insights and freedom that came to me. It was a giant step forward in the wisdom spoken of in the Proverbs telling us that the fear of God is the beginning of wisdom. It enabled me to see more clearly than ever before how the fear of man had impacted my life and how it plays a major role in our interactions with others. Our success in finding The Love Connection and continuing on to see it completed is determined by the focus of our fear—is it on God or man?

THE PRINCE OF PEACE

Jesus had strong feelings about this fear of man and how deceptive it can be. He said:

> Do not think I came to bring peace on earth. I did not come to bring peace but a sword. For I have come to "set a man against his father, a daughter against her mother, and a daughter-in-law against her mother-in-law"; and "a man's enemies will be those of his own household." He who loves father or mother more than Me is not worthy of Me. And he who loves son or daughter more than Me is not worthy of Me.
>
> —MATTHEW 10:34–37

"But wait a minute. Isn't Jesus the Prince of Peace? And aren't we supposed to love our parents, our spouses, and our children?"

What's the worst thing an enemy can do to us? Nine times out of ten, people reply, "He can kill us." However, Jesus said we shouldn't fear those who can only kill us, we should just fear the One "who is able to destroy both body and soul in hell" (Matt. 10:28); and that's not the devil. But, getting back to the question, what is the worst thing an enemy can do to us? The worst thing an enemy can do to us is to come between us and God. We allow that to happen when we're more fearful of losing others' approval than losing His.

A guy can get up some morning to find that his wife isn't speaking to him. He might ask her what is wrong and what he has done that offended her. No matter how nicely he might ask or how much he assures her that if he had hurt her, he was certainly unaware of what he did. All day long he could keep reviewing the events and conversations he had with his wife that may have upset her. He could ask himself again and again what he should have done or should have said to avoid this unfortunate turn of events.

That evening as he evaluates his day, he might find he had spent five hours agonizing over what may have displeased his wife and about five minutes being concerned about whether or not he had displeased God. Who was most important to him that day?

Who makes the best husband or wife; one who is more fearful of losing their spouse's approval, or one who is fearful of losing God's approval? How can a wife or husband who is more fearful of losing their mate's approval speak the things in love that need to be said for the sake of a healthy love relationship? God's counsel has been well tested and proven over the centuries—the fear of God is the beginning of wisdom.

In counseling sessions and in everyday encounters with people, I have been amazed at how we can be so fearful of doing something we know is right and good just because we fear losing the approval of family members. We are born attached by an umbilical cord to our mother. For both the child's and the mother's survival, someone needs to cut the cord. Family and relatives can be very helpful, but not when we allow them to get in between us and God. So Jesus, the Prince of Peace, brings a sword to cut us free from unhealthy relationship ties, and by doing so He blesses us with peace.

Religious Correctness

The desire to be politically correct is one of the strongest detrimental influences on our nation's political, moral, and economic condition today. The most common attitude of our population in the earlier years of our nation was marked by the desire to look good in God's eyes. America's Founding Fathers, who sacrificed their lives and fortunes to establish a nation under God, were far more fearful of losing God's approval than they were of losing man's approval. A return to the fear of God would take all the wind out of the sails of the boat called "political correctness."

This very harmful attitude which is so prevalent in secular realms has also infiltrated the church as "religious correctness." This may account for some of the weakness we see in the body of Christ today. We need to return to the place where wisdom begins—the fear of God.

One way this religious correctness shows up is in what Jesus called "the tradition of men." Jesus rebuked the

Pharisees and scribes, saying they were setting aside the commandments of God in order to keep their tradition, the traditions of men (see Mark 7:8–9). Their concern for pleasing religious leaders obviously was given a higher priority than pleasing God. The traditions of men have been around for a long time and are still with us today because fear of man is still with us.

In seminary I had the privilege of studying the Old Testament under a wonderful man of God who was highly regarded, both for his biblical scholarship and his godly character. In his classroom lectures, he would get powerfully motivated by his love for God and his deep respect for the Bible as he passionately presented biblical truths he felt were so important for us to embrace.

His reverence for God's words and his passion for accurately preserving them were seen in a special moment in class. He told of how he had a part in working on a new version of the Bible. He brought his translation of a particular passage to the prestigious director of the project. The director agreed that his translation was more accurate and much better than the most widely used translation of that time, but he decided to stay with the older version. With a display of righteous indignation that I'll probably never forget, he painfully repeated the director's reason: people have grown accustomed to the current version.

We need to take special care in our handling of the Scriptures to responsibly translate God's words. We are able to do this if our fear of not pleasing Him is greater than our fear of not pleasing men. Wanting to please God requires our seeking to understand Him more fully. And that, in turn, makes it imperative that we have accurate knowledge of what He has said.

"But, wait a minute. Why all the fuss? Don't we have reliable versions of the Bible today that are accurate translations done by top biblical scholars?"

It's certainly true that over the centuries many godly, dedicated scholars have worked diligently to give us the best translations. However, very early in the process the traditions of men began creeping in so that today we see some of the most important words of Christ have become ambiguous and the power of His message is blunted.

The good news is that we can use literal translations of the original Greek texts of the New Testament to reveal the clearest, most reliable words of Christ. Large portions of these texts were written by Matthew and John, who were actual witnesses to His words. And the rest was written by men who were close to the events they recorded. The first Bible translations, on the other hand, were made hundreds of years after the original texts were written.

Thankfully, some Bible versions give the literal meanings of key words in their marginal notes. But if you wish to pursue this issue any further than what is done here, there are many Bible study tools available today that can be very helpful. Some are even free on the Internet. All that is needed, however, is a Strong's Concordance or a Greek English interlinear Bible.

A rather simple but effective guideline for testing the validity of literal meanings is an ancient adage, "The Greeks have a word for it." Because the Greeks seem to have a word for every nuance of a word's meaning, they don't have to make a word serve with two different meanings. They have such a precise vocabulary that it is widely used for medical and scientific terms.

So we will see that the best literal translation for a word

is usually the one that makes the best spiritual and logical sense when it is consistently used for that word in each passage where it is found. Let's do a brief word study, using this approach to see how we can discern the clear message of the gospel. In this particular study, we will see God's priorities more clearly presented. But without a literal translation, it's easy for God's priorities to get reshuffled.

GOD'S PRIORITIES

When Jesus had encounters with people, wonderful things happened to them, like what happened to four people who are described in the Book of Luke. One of these was the lady who washed the feet of Jesus with her tears (7:50). Another was the lady with a flow of blood (8:48). Then there was the Samaritan leper who returned to give thanks (17:19). And there was also the blind man whose sight was restored (18:42).

In the accounts of these people written by Luke, who was a physician, we see that their stories were quite different from each other, yet they all had one very important thing in common—they all were born again. Each time Jesus said the same thing to each one to emphasize what was so special about what had just happened in their life—His literal words were, "Your faith has saved you."

This is what most versions show Jesus saying to the woman who washed His feet with her tears, yet to the other three, most versions show Jesus saying, "Your faith has made you whole," "Your faith has made you well," or "Your faith has healed you."

When a person hasn't yet met the Lord, the most important thing that could possibly happen to them is to encounter Jesus Christ and receive Him as Lord. So wouldn't this be what Jesus was most eager to announce to each one of them? Let's examine the account of the leper for more insight on this question.

> Now it happened as He went to Jerusalem that He passed through the midst of Samaria and Galilee. Then as He entered a certain village, there met Him ten men who were lepers, who stood afar off. And they lifted up their voices and said, "Jesus, Master, have mercy on us!" So when He saw them, He said to them, "Go, show yourselves to the priests." And so it was that as they went, they were cleansed. And one of them, when he saw that he was healed, returned, and with a loud voice glorified God, and fell down on his face at His feet, giving Him thanks. And he was a Samaritan. So Jesus answered and said, "Were there not ten cleansed? But where are the nine? "Were there not any found who returned to give glory to God except this foreigner?" And He said to him, "Arise, go your way, Your faith has [saved] you."
>
> —Luke 17:11–19

(Note: in this book, brackets indicate where a scriptural quotation has been changed with a literal translation.)

There are three very significant words in the original Greek texts of this account. We can compare them by seeing them spelled with English letters and followed by their literal translations. The first one is *katharizo*, meaning "cleansed." And the second one is *iaomai*, meaning "healed." All ten lepers were cleansed and healed, but Jesus used a different word, *sozo*, meaning "saved," for the one who returned to give glory to God. He must have deliberately chosen this particular word because in addition to healing, this leper received something else of much greater value than physical healing—he received eternal life.

And that's the same special thing that happened to the lady who had washed His feet with her tears. There's no mention of healing, but she also had a *sozo* experience just like the leper had. So Jesus told her what He also told the leper, "Your faith has saved you."

When we use the literal translation, "saved," God's number one priority is properly expressed. His gift of salvation is always more precious than any kind of physical healing. His constant, number one priority is either to bring us into or to bring us closer in loving relationship with Him—that's the eternal life He offers. Jesus said, "If your hand or foot causes you to sin, cut it off and cast it from you. It is better for you to enter into life lame or maimed, rather than having two hands or two feet, to be cast into the everlasting fire" (Matt. 18:8).

The proper priority of faith is also illustrated here. Salvation wouldn't have been possible for these four if they had not believed that they needed forgiveness and that Jesus had the authority to forgive. Fully meeting these two requirements of faith can produce a deep down, thorough washing of forgiveness that may erupt with an open display of joy and thankfulness. Jesus pointed this out to Simon, the Pharisee:

> Then He turned to the woman and said to Simon, "Do you see this woman? I entered your house; you gave Me no water for My feet, but she has washed My feet with her tears and wiped them with the hair of her head. You gave Me no kiss, but this woman has not ceased to kiss My feet since the time I came in. You did not anoint My head with

oil, but this woman has anointed My feet with fragrant oil. Therefore I say to you, her sins, which are many, are forgiven, for she loved much. But to whom little is forgiven, the same loves little." Then He said to the woman, "Your faith has saved you. Go in peace."

—LUKE 7:44–47, 50

We also see the faith for salvation in the lady with the flow of blood. She must have felt both the need to be saved and that Jesus had the authority to forgive. She said to herself, "If only I may touch His garment, I shall be [saved]" (Matt. 9:21). In Luke's account, she declares to Jesus "in the presence of all the people the reason she had touched Him and how she was healed immediately" (Luke 8:47). There were two parts to her declaration: the reason she touched Him and the fact that she was healed. She touched Him for salvation; but then, probably startled by the awesome power that was working in her body, "she came trembling" with her account of a surprise bonus gift.

Someone can be exceedingly glad and excited over being healed. But it's when the healing experience leads to salvation that someone is able to freely glorify God like we saw the blind man doing.

> And immediately he received his sight, and followed Him, glorifying God. And all the people, when they saw it, gave praise to God.
>
> —LUKE 18:43

Needless to say, both faith and healing are extremely valuable, so we will make a further investigation of these a little later. What we've just seen, however, is the highest priority for the use of our faith—that's for our being saved.

This rescues us from the "everlasting fire"; but the really good news is that it brings us out of loneliness into the wonderful warmth of God's love, the distinguishing mark of TLC. So these four met the author of salvation—they found The Love Connection!

If you haven't found it, I urge you right now to accept this challenge of a lifetime by praying a simple, sincere prayer like the following:

> *God, I have resisted Your love and have gone my own independent way. I now ask Jesus, whom You raised from the dead, to be the Lord of my life. Forgive me for my sins; I accept the death of Jesus as full payment for all my sins. I give my life to You. Shape me and mold me to be all that You have called me to be. Thank You.*

Chapter 3

PROTECTING THE LOVE CONNECTION

All things have become new.

F inding TLC means a bunch of extraordinary things
have happened to you, if you just prayed that prayer.
But this is what has happened to all Christians.
Most amazingly, we no longer have an I-nature. Instead of
being separated from God, we now can have the special love
relationship with God like a child can have with an earthly
father who is truly loving and caring. This is because of the
phenomenal changes that have taken place. We've passed
from death into life by being spiritually reborn from above.
We've been transferred from the kingdom of darkness into
the kingdom of God, and we have been made one spirit
with Him and all the others in the body of Christ. Truly
"old things have passed away; behold, all things have become
new" (2 Cor. 5:17).

The greatest advantage we gain from the born-again
experience is a wonderful, brand-new, deeper sense of being
loved and having a greater, overall feeling of love for others.
Above all else, this is what makes TLC worth everything.
Still, The Challenge remains there before us, always challenging us to complete TLC but now, also confronting us

with the task of protecting at all cost what we have gained in The Love Connection.

All things have become new, but we are still in the throes of a cosmic conflict. Our enemy failed to keep us independent and apart from God. As a matter of fact, the I-nature that had dominated our soul is no more. We now have a "New nature" that has welcomed Jesus Christ as our Lord and Savior and wants to be more like Him.

Nevertheless, regardless of how dramatic our change may have been at salvation, we soon realize that while the traits of the I-nature may have been seriously subdued, they still survived. Now they continue as a part of our soul, operating as a law unto themselves, which we will call the "Old nature." It exists right along with the "New" in an ongoing rivalry as long as we are on this earth. However, we can be strongly encouraged today with the same encouragement Paul gave the Philippians, "Being confident of this very thing, that He who has begun a good work in you will complete it until the day of Jesus Christ" (Phil. 1:6).

Because of the Old nature, we continue to be vulnerable to the world's schemes; and to the extent of its dominance in our soul, it keeps us from having fullness of joy. In the most subtle and deceitful ways, it is continually working to separate us from TLC. This Old nature and its traits just can't be ignored; something has to be done about it if we are to protect and complete TLC. Look at Paul's admission of his struggle with it. He had a remarkable born-again experience, yet years later he was still contending with this problem, which he described as "another law in my members."

> For the good that I will to do, I do not do; but the evil I will not to do, that I practice. Now if I will

to do what I will not to do, it is no longer I who
do it, but sin that dwells in me. I find then a law,
that evil is present with me, the one who wills to
do good. For I delight in the law of God according
to the inward man. But I see another law in my
members, warring against the law of my mind, and
bringing me into captivity to the law of sin which
is in my members.

—ROMANS 7:19–23

JESUS, OUR BEST EXAMPLE

The good news is that Jesus, who is our best example in
everything, overcame this "law" in His members instead
of allowing the world to conform Him. He gave us a very
convincing example of His own life so we may have hope
and faith to believe it's also possible for us to do the same.
Before leaving this world, He said to His disciples, "In the
world you will have tribulation; but be of good cheer, I have
overcome the world" (John 16:33).

Later, as John wrote about his vision on the Isle of
Patmos, we see how Jesus encourages us in this overcoming
with the most extraordinary incentives imaginable. He
starts off with some really good rewards, such as: "To him
who overcomes I will give to eat from the tree of life, which
is in the midst of the Paradise of God" (Rev. 2:7). After
offering several other more extravagant rewards, He throws
in the whole works with one final, grand offer: "To him who
overcomes I will grant to sit with Me on My throne, as I
also overcame and sat down with My Father on His throne"
(Rev. 3:21). Now that's a highly exhilarating thought! Could
He possibly mean that this is for the likes of you and me?
Yes, and I'm convinced He's totally sincere and will surely
deliver as promised.

When Jesus was on this earth as a man, He had to contend with His *Old* nature just like we have to, which is why it was possible that He "was in all points tempted as we are" (Heb. 4:15). The big difference is that He never sinned like all of us have. (See Hebrews 2:17–18; Romans 3:23.) Let's have a closer look at how the world seeks to overcome us with its temptations. Then we'll look at how Jesus overcame the world, and how we can follow His example.

The enemy is always seductively maneuvering for a chance to hook us by the warped desires of our *Old* nature. Once he gets us hooked, he tries to drag us away, stealing us from Him who we rightfully belong to. And, of course, his intention is to utterly destroy us if he can get by with it (John 10:10). James, the brother of Jesus, describes temptation like this:

> Let no one say when he is tempted, "I am tempted by God"; for God cannot be tempted by evil, nor does He Himself tempt anyone. But each one is tempted when he is drawn away by his own desires and enticed. Then, when desire has conceived, it gives birth to sin; and sin, when it is full-grown, brings forth death.
>
> —JAMES 1:13–15

The *Old* nature resists the things of God, especially our God-given desires. So it comes up with its own twisted desires, vainly attempting in a roundabout way to satisfy our God-given desires without TLC. This makes us vulnerable to the world's temptations, which, of course, don't get us the love our heart truly longs for. The wisdom of Proverbs speaks to this condition: "There is a way that seems right to a man, But its end is the way of death" (Prov. 16:25). When our *Old* nature dominates our soul, our whole perspective on life is warped. That's when these words of God are so true:

> "For My thoughts are not your thoughts, Nor are your ways My ways," says the LORD. "For as the heavens are higher than the earth, So are My ways higher than your ways, And My thoughts than your thoughts."
>
> —ISAIAH 55:8–9

How Jesus Overcame

Jesus was able to overcome the world and its lusts because He was willing to lay down His soul with its *Old* nature for a complete restoration. About a thousand years before Jesus, David wrote of this process in his life: "The LORD is my shepherd; I shall not want.... He restores my soul; He leads me in the paths of righteousness For His name's sake" (Ps. 23:1, 3).

Jesus overcame the world by daily "losing" His soul's *Old* nature so that eventually He had totally put it to death. This is what He was telling the disciples on the way to His crucifixion: "I will no longer talk much with you, for the ruler of this world is coming, and he has nothing in Me" (John 14:30).

Everything the enemy might have had a chance to get a hold of in Jesus was now gone. His soul had been completely restored to a soul "filled with all the fullness of God" (Eph. 3:19), so that it became totally dominated by a *New* nature.

> Therefore I will divide Him a portion with the great, And He shall divide the spoil with the strong, Because He poured out His soul unto death, And He was numbered with the transgressors, And He

bore the sin of many, And made intercession for
the transgressors.
—Isaiah 53:12

Therefore God also has highly exalted Him and
given Him the name which is above every name.
—Philippians 2:9

There is no better way for us to protect and complete
TLC than by following the example of Jesus in laying down
our soul. And God is our best help in the process because
He's always intent on gathering us into a closer bond of love
with Him. And once we've found Jesus, TLC, the Father
is able to draw us closer because Jesus is the "Way" to the
Father. "Jesus said to him, 'I am the way, the truth, and the
life. No one comes to the Father except through Me'" (John
14:6). That's when God immediately becomes more proac-
tive in directing our steps for this purpose. And it's good
that He's always working for our best interests, because,
after all, He's the One who controls everything.

The Great Arranger

If there is going to be any meaningful restoring of our soul,
God is the One, and the only One, who could ever bring it
about. We're totally dependent on Him, or it never happens.
No matter how convincing the claims may sound, there
is no other person or program that has the possibility of
accomplishing this kind of complete change.

Here's why God is "The Great Arranger." No other
person could possibly arrange the intricate details of our life
in such a way that all things work together toward that end.
He's the One who leads us in the path of restoration. And
He does it "for His name's sake" (1 John 2:12) because there

is no way for us to earn it or deserve it. While He's leading us and arranging things, what would be the ideal picture in His mind of a completed job? With His intention always being to draw us into the closest love relationship possible, we have only one answer—Jesus. He's the ideal model for that closeness because He and the Father are one. Paul describes The Arranger's extensive training program:

> And we know that all things work together for good to those who love God, to those who are the called according to His purpose. For whom He foreknew, He also predestined to be conformed to the image of His Son, that He might be the first-born among many brethren.
> —ROMANS 8:28–29

Jesus said,

> A disciple is not above his teacher, but everyone who is [completely] trained will be like his teacher.
> —LUKE 6:40

At the beginning I said The Challenge is absolutely the most demanding, most exciting, and most rewarding of all challenges. Now we'll see why that's true, because continuing with it challenges us to follow Jesus. We've been informed of the rewards for following Him and how God so very well arranges everything for that purpose. Now let's consider the demands put upon us when we're following Jesus; and then we'll look more specifically at our part in the process.

FOLLOWING JESUS

But how do we even begin to do as He did? Actually, He is very helpful in showing us how. Better than any teacher or leader the world's ever known, Jesus practiced what He preached. The biblical record shows Him living as the perfect example for us. But then, He also explained with a few simple words how to do as He did:

> Then Jesus said to His disciples, "If anyone desires to come after Me, let him deny himself and take up his cross, and follow Me. For whoever desires to save his [soul] will lose it, but whoever loses his [soul] for My sake will find it. For what profit is it to a man if he gains the whole world, and loses his own soul? Or what will a man give in exchange for his soul?"
>
> —MATTHEW 16:24–26

If we wish to have the full impact of what Jesus is teaching here so we can know the freedom and joy that comes from acting on it, we will want to know the literal meaning of His words. So let's take time for a short word study.

Earlier we looked at some of the advantages of literal translations and the usefulness of the adage "The Greeks have a word for it." With these in mind, we see another instance where we don't have to use two different meanings for the same Greek word. This helps us to grasp a most vital point that Jesus is making here.

The Greek word Jesus spoke in this passage is *psuche*, which is literally translated "soul." However, in verse 25 we usually see most versions translate it "life." Jesus obviously had a good reason for His deliberate use of the Greek word that means "soul." This word *psuche* is where we get our words "psychology" and "psyche," which Webster's dictionary defines as "The soul or spirit...the center of thought, feeling, and behavior."

Now the Greeks do have a word for life: *zoe*, which is where we get our word "zoology." This would have been a logical choice of words if Jesus had wanted to talk about physical life. But that was not the case; a consistent translation of *soul* in both verses 25 and 26 makes the best logical and spiritual sense of this passage. This clearly expresses God's priorities and intentions—He's looking for more than just an outward change of lifestyle.

Our Soul Is Us

Denying one's self is denying the *Old* part of one's soul that resists following Jesus. This is the way we find our soul—the restored soul that makes possible a right relationship with God and others. Essentially, we can say, "My soul is me: It's my self-image, how I want people to see me. But it's also my secret hopes and dreams, my fears, my strongest desires, my pride, and all my cover-ups." Our soul, which houses all these facets of "me," lives forever and is far dearer to us than our physical life. This fact is often revealed in a Freudian slip, when someone makes a remark like, "I'll die before I'll ever ask that guy for anything!" It's possible to allow self interests to become more important than hanging on to our physical life; otherwise, no one would ever commit suicide.

Peter's story very well illustrates what's happening in our soul. With the literal translation of *soul* in John 13:37–38, we see Peter telling Jesus he was willing to follow Him even at the greatest cost:

> "I will lay down my [soul] for Your sake." Jesus answered him, "Will you lay down your [soul] for

My sake? Most assuredly, I say to you, the rooster
shall not crow till you have denied Me three times."

A short time later, Jesus and His disciples with their two
swords were met by a large force of men, well equipped
with weapons, coming to arrest Jesus. Peter was willing to
take them all on and started swinging his sword. He wasn't
afraid of laying his physical life on the line.

But then, not long after, when Peter's *Old* nature was
threatened with possibly being ridiculed for knowing Jesus,
he denied he knew Him three times. He was unable to
lay down his soul for Jesus' sake. Laying down our soul is
much harder than laying down our physical life. The literal
translation reveals the demands of a God who is motivated
by pure love and for our best interests. Consequently, He
desires a radical change, deeper than any change of outward
appearance. So He commands us, "You shall love the LORD
your God with all your heart, with all your soul, and with
all your mind" (Matt 22:37).

Following Jesus is summed up in this: "For whoever
desires to save his [soul] will lose it, but whoever loses his
[soul] for My sake will find it" (Matt. 16:25). How can you
find something by losing it? If we want to have the kind of
soul God wants us to have, we have to be willing to let go
of, or "lose," any part of our soul that is dominated by the
Old nature. We call this putting off the *Old* nature and putting on the *New*. Paul calls them "old man" (Col. 3:9) and
"new man" (v. 10). We are putting off and putting on for the
sake of Jesus and His purposes, although there isn't anything else we could ever do that even comes close to being
as good as that is for our own self-interests.

You encounter a little puppy dog with a poison bone in
his mouth. He looks pitifully thin and neglected, sitting

there, gripping the bone very tightly as though it's the most precious thing he's ever had. You love little puppy dogs and you are right now flooded with tender sympathy for this one here in front of you. You feel you have to get that poison bone out of its mouth. You move a little closer, positioning yourself to grab the bone; but the puppy senses your intentions, draws back, and appears ready to run.

You wisely conclude that he thinks you might try to take away this very choice goody. So you quickly devise a different strategy. You pull out of your bag one of the fresh steak strips you just bought at the market and hold it out to the puppy. You're thinking, *If I can just get this steak close enough for him to get a good whiff, he will drop the poison bone and go for the steak.* Finally, you've edged close enough and you can see his eyes darting back and forth between you and the steak. But the story ends here with a question—will the puppy go for the steak or will he run away with his "precious" possession?

CHANGE

When we are on The Challenge's lifelong quest to complete TLC, or when we are aspiring to do any notable thing in God's kingdom, we will need to be open to radical change. Surviving any attack against our love relationship with God is always possible if we are willing to abandon our self-interests and lay down our soul for Him. In spite of all the good reasons, this kind of change isn't a piece of cake.

There's an attitude that can sometimes be found loitering in the shadowy places of our mind. When it finds a chink in our armor, it tells us, "You don't need to change! You need to hold on to the *Old* nature for your own best interests. Sure, there are a few things you could probably improve on a little bit, but the real problem is the way everybody else is messing everything up. A lot of those other guys out there really need to get their act together, but you don't need any more of that *New* nature stuff. And even now there are a lot of people who think you've already gone too far out with this religious business."

As we are following Jesus, it will become quite apparent that we will have to deal boldly with the *Old* nature; otherwise this part of our soul that's so attracted to the world will always be trying to draw us into some ugly situation. But something is going to give, either the *Old* or the *New*. Consequently, we have to be willing to bravely face the raw realities of life. However, if our *Old* nature with its fancy footwork has already convinced us to settle for where we presently are with God and our neighbor, and we are unaware of any major discontent within our soul, then we're not very likely to think of changing. So, Jesus admonishes us, "He who loves his [soul] will lose it, and he who hates his [soul] in this world will keep it for eternal life" (John 12:25).

But the good news is there are some who wish to follow Christ regardless of the cost. "And from the days of John the Baptist until now the kingdom of heaven suffers violence, and the violent take it by force" (Matt. 11:12). There's a beneficial kind of suffering; it's like what a rock endures in a rock tumbler. We all are rough and unfinished, so our entering into fellowship with other believers is like jumping into the tumbler where we will be bumped and whacked by one another's rough edges until someday we may be a polished, bright gem for His crown. "As iron sharpens iron, So a man sharpens the countenance of his friend" (Prov. 27:17).

John and Billy came to the Boy Scout meeting a little

late that night. That was a no-no because they were supposed to be learning responsibility. To the scoutmaster, that
was bad enough, but in addition their uniforms were torn
and they looked totally disheveled. The scoutmaster sternly
asked them to give an account for their sad condition. John
said, "Me and Billy were on our way to the meeting tonight
when we got a chance to do a good deed. We helped a little
old lady cross the street. But it was really hard. To begin
with, she's a lot tougher than she looks, and then she fought
us all the way till we got'er across the street. That's when we
figured it out—she didn't want to cross the street!"

Sometimes we see folks get a little misguided in their sincere intentions to help us; that just comes with the fellowship package. Yet, the fact remains, our *Old* nature is a lot
tougher than it looks, and it wants to stay right where it
is. The Great Arranger can have us in a situation where we
have to make a hard choice between pleasing God or our
Old nature; that's when our soul can become gravely con-
flicted. This is where we see the Ultimate Survivors shine.
They are the "violent" who take the kingdom by force, "crucifying the flesh" (see Galatians 5:24)—but that's a good
kind of self-inflicted violence. "For if you live according to
the flesh you will die; but if by the Spirit you put to death
the deeds of the body you will live" (Rom. 8:13).

An all-out surrender to God's will may do such violence
against our *Old* nature that it can bring an unsettling sense
of something dying deep inside our soul. David likens this
experience to walking "through the valley of the shadow of
death" (Ps. 23:4). But this kind of dying is a good thing; it's
not death like the end of life—it's just the shadow of death.
This walk can so change us that we can reach a place where
we're then able to sit down and enjoy banqueting at a table

God prepares for us right in the presence of our enemies, in the presence of the challenges that used to crush us.

On the other hand, if we choose to hold on to the *Old* nature, that's when the consequences can become woefully tragic. And we might do some pretty awful things, give up on life altogether, or live on with bitterness, blaming God and others for our discontentment. But look at Jesus. He had many hard choices, like when it was time for Him to go to the cross. The struggle in His soul was so intense that He sweated blood. Then, as always, He was a perfect example for us. A few days earlier when He could see it coming, He said, "Now My soul is troubled, and what shall I say? 'Father, save Me from this hour'? But for this purpose I came to this hour. Father, glorify Your name" (John 12:27–28).

And right now even as you are reading this, you may be facing a very troubling situation. Nonetheless, in all things, always, God wants you to have bright hopes and expectations. This is obviously what carried Jesus through all of His challenges. Can we be more specific about what it was that enabled Him to abandon all self-interests and lay down His soul in the most shameful, horrendous death, "even the death of the cross" (Phil. 2:8)? Even though He despised the shame of the cross, yet He endured it "for the joy that was set before Him" (Heb. 12:2). Jesus was expecting a joy so magnificent, so desirable above all treasures, that He willing accepted the agony that was the pathway to the joy.

The Process

So if this joy set before Him was good enough to carry Jesus through the most horrendous ordeal in all of history, wouldn't our having that kind of joy be more than adequate to carry us through the worst of our trials? This kind of joy isn't the giggly, superficial sort. It's a deep down, secure feeling that knows that God loves me, and He has the best plan for my life. The path that leads us into His special kind of joy is laid out in the "vine talk" where Jesus gave us an excellent description of the process that God uses to bring about beautiful changes in us:

> I am the true vine, and My Father is the vine-dresser. Every branch in Me that does not bear fruit He takes away; and every branch that bears fruit He prunes, that it may bear more fruit. You are already clean because of the word which I have spoken to you. Abide in Me, and I in you. As the branch cannot bear fruit of itself, unless it abides in the vine, neither can you, unless you abide in Me.
>
> I am the vine, you are the branches. He who abides Me, and I in him, bears much fruit; for without Me you can do nothing. If anyone does not abide in Me, he is cast out as a branch and is withered; and they gather them and throw them into the fire, and they are burned. If you abide in Me, and My words abide in you, you will ask what you desire, and it shall be done for you. By this My Father is glorified, that you bear much fruit; so you will be My disciples.
>
> As the Father loved Me, I also have loved you; abide in My love. If you keep My commandments, you will abide in My love, just as I have kept My Father's commandments and abide in His love.
>
> These things I have spoken to you, that My joy may remain in you, and that your joy may be full. This is My commandment that you love one another as I have loved you. Greater love has no

one than this, than to lay down one's [soul] for his friends.

—JOHN 15:1–13

Jesus had earlier described this process of change in a general fashion when He spoke of it as losing our soul for His sake (see Matthew 16:24–27). Here He gives the particulars of the process, saying it's to "lay down one's [soul] for his friends" (John 15:13). Paul calls it "chastening." "If you endure chastening, God deals with you as with sons; for what son is there whom a father does not chasten?" (Heb. 12:7). James describes the process as "various trials." "My brethren, count it all joy when you fall into various trials" (James 1:2). And David calls it the "path of life." "You will show me the path of life; In Your presence is fullness of joy; At Your right hand are pleasures forevermore" (Ps. 16:11).

While joy is a sure indication we are pleasing God, it also reveals His nature. The fact of His providing a path to that joy shows His love for us. If you sincerely love someone, don't you want their joy to be full? Here are the steps in this path which we see presented in the Vine Talk:

1. We choose to please God and obey His commandment to love (John 15:12).

2. The greatest love we can give is laying down our soul for our friends (v. 13).

3. We can only do this by abiding in Him so we can endure the pruning that's required (vv. 1–8).

4. Obeying Him keeps us abiding in Him and His love (vv. 9–10).

5. His joy is made full in us when we submit to
   His directions (v. 11).

All the important particulars of the process come together when we surrender to the pruning by laying down our soul. This is a very difficult thing to do, which, no doubt, is why He said, "Greater love has no one than this" (v. 13). However, everyone who is abiding in Him gets pruned because that's what happens on the "path of life." It's being "chastened" by the "various trials" The Arranger has allowed because of His deep love for us.

Ultimate Survivors call these "pruning opportunities" because these are where the *Old* traits can be put off when we choose to put on the *New*, which, in turn, enables us to overcome the trial. It's "pulling down strongholds" (2 Cor. 10:4) that resist our knowing God. The *Old* nature that hinders our fellowship with God is being replaced with the *New*, which means we are being more conformed to the image of His Son so that more fruit of the Spirit...love, joy, and peace (vv. 2, 8) is seen in us.

Who Gets the Glory?

Someone may ask, "What was Jesus after, anyway? What were His motives?" Of course, He always said what His Father wanted Him to say, but did He also have good reasons of His own for saying what He said here? When He was on this earth, what did He repeatedly demonstrate was the uppermost motive in all His actions? Wasn't it His first desire to please His Father in all that He did so His Father would get the glory?

We see this, for example, when He promised the disciples that He would do whatever their request; His intention in responding would always be "that the Father may be glorified in the Son" (John 14:13). So too in John 15:8, His purpose for wanting us to follow His example of laying down His soul is that it will glorify His Father.

Don't we find this to be true; the one we are most eager to see get the glory is the one we are most eager to please? Whom do you wish to please? Whom do you want to see glorified?

Could our success in surviving the process simply boil down to rightly choosing who it is we want to receive the glory and whom we want to please? Or, how much of the glory do I need for me and how much do I want to go to God?

"But wait a minute! Isn't it right that God should get all the glory?"

Yes! But why? One good reason—the glory is His. The whole thing belongs to Him, "For Yours is the kingdom and the power and the glory forever. Amen" (Matt. 6:13). It's extraordinarily loving that He shares these with us, but they belong to Him.

Yet, there's another excellent reason. When we're doing anything to please God with the intent that He gets all the glory, that's when you can be absolutely confident the results will be the very best for everyone involved. First off, it will be best for God because it's being done according to His will and therefore it's accomplishing His foremost desire of drawing us into a closer love relationship with Him. But that means it's also best for us because being closer to Him brings us into more of Him.

In short, the process produces good or bad results, depending on whom we are choosing to please. David urges us to choose God. "Oh, taste and see that the LORD is good;

Blessed is the man who trusts in Him" (Ps. 34:8)! The joy of God's presence that we receive when we're pleasing Him becomes more satisfying all the time. Someday we may come to say like David, "Your loving kindness is better than life" (63:3). The hinge upon which the entire process of change swings: living to please God or self?

We have seen how joy plays a major part in our protecting The Love Connection. Now, as we continue in The Challenge, we will not be leaving joy behind, for it is essential in our goal of completing TLC.

Chapter 4

COMPLETING THE LOVE CONNECTION

A Goal and the Way to the Goal

W hy has The Challenge—the greatest of all challenges—continually pointed us toward the goal of completing The Love Connection? No goal is worthwhile for you or me or for anyone if it isn't also a goal that God has. Well, we can be absolutely sure that our being in closest love relationship with Him is uppermost in God's mind; and certainly TLC is just that! However, what we want to know are the essential specifics of the TLC in its completion that make it so important to God so we have the clearest picture of where we're headed.

One year while I was in college, I was on the way to a summer job in Alaska. The last leg of the journey was in an old rickety, amphibian passenger plane. It was a stormy day with very poor visibility, but I was enjoying the adventuresome moment. I was sitting up close to the pilot, who didn't seem to mind answering my questions, so we easily became engaged in an interesting conversation about the challenges of flying in those conditions.

At one point, a view of the airport we were headed for appeared on the instrument panel. I asked, "How is it that we can see the airport there but we don't see it looking through the windows? Is this a special kind of radar or camera?" "Oh no," he said. "This is just an illuminated picture of the airport so we'll know we're coming into the right airport when we see something that matches this picture.

Having our goal in The Challenge clearly illuminated helps us select the route and make the necessary preparations that will bring us into our special landing field. First, a brief word study should help us to frame the picture. We need to determine precisely what is meant by the word *complete*. The persistent problem we've been dealing with all along is the *Old* nature we've inherited. The ultimate solution must be to replace it with a *New* nature modeled after Jesus; which we have observed, after all, is precisely God's agenda. Isn't it then quite logical to say someone is "complete" when their *Old* nature has been "completely" replaced with the *New?* In this sense "complete" is well described with Paul's admonition to be "filled with all the fullness of God" (Eph. 3:19).

This also must have been the goal James was talking about. There's only one possible way to be "complete" and "lacking nothing"—that's to be filled with the fullness of God.

> My brethren, count it all joy when you fall into various trials, knowing that the testing of your faith produces [endurance]. But let [endurance] have its [complete] work, that you may be [complete] and [entire], lacking nothing.
> —JAMES 1:2–4

The word "complete" appears to be the best literal translation here of the Greek word *teleios*, which is defined as "complete" in Strong's Concordance. This word is commonly found translated in most versions as "perfect," which in our English usage today usually conveys the notion of being without any faults or defects. The Greek language of the New Testament, however, had a better word for "perfect," if that would have been the intended meaning; it was *amomos*, translated "without blemish" or "faultless." Also, the translation of "complete" is supported by the fact that it consistently fits better in most passages. For example:

> But when that which is [complete] has come, then that which is in part will be done away.
> —1 CORINTHIANS 13:10

> Till we all come to the unity of the faith and of the knowledge of the Son of God, to a [complete] man, to the measure of the stature of the fullness of Christ.
> —EPHESIANS 4:13

Perhaps the best reason for preferring "complete" is that even if we could validate the use of "perfect," the notion of a person being perfect, or without fault, would be impossible unless that person was completely full of God.

FILLED WITH ALL THE FULLNESS OF GOD

Jesus commands us, "Therefore you shall be [complete], just as your Father in heaven is [complete]" (Matt. 5:48). Paul told the believers in Colossae that he labored to the end "that we may present every man [complete] in Christ Jesus" (Col. 1:28). And the letter to the Hebrews urges us, "Therefore, leaving the discussion of the elementary principles of Christ, let us go on to [completion]" (Heb. 6:1).

Obviously, this is a primary goal for true followers of Jesus Christ. It's hard to imagine a follower of Christ consciously choosing a goal of something other than being completely filled with God. That would be like never wanting to be any more than just partly filled with the fullness of God. Isn't that like saying, "I only want to be partly filled with the joy of the Lord"? Or, "I only want to see His will partly done on earth as it is in heaven"?

"But, wait a minute. If I'm filled with the fullness of God, will I be like a little play soldier, just one of many look-alike tin soldiers all in a row? Does it mean I lose my uniqueness, my individuality?"

On the contrary, God wants to reveal Himself through the uniqueness of your *New* nature. Remember, He's the One who deliberately made your fingerprints different from everybody else's. But that shouldn't surprise us because He is so delighted to show His love to each part of His creation—even a falling snowflake has reason to praise God and glorify Him through its being different from all the others.

In our completeness the hope of our calling is realized and our uniqueness is fully expressed. This was the goal of Paul's pressing on; he wanted to get a hold of whatever it was that Christ Jesus had in mind for him. "Not that I have already [obtained], or am already [completed]; but I press on, that I may lay hold of that for which Christ Jesus has also laid hold of me" (Phil. 3:12). So it is with Ultimate Survivors; their goal is always looking beyond the trial of survival at hand—always reaching to ultimately fulfill God's highest calling for their life.

Now we're getting a general picture of our goal. And it's quite apparent that no person on earth at this time is completely filled with the fullness of God. Nevertheless, we can encourage each other like Paul did because we too are "being confident of this very thing, that He who has begun a good work in you will complete it until the day of Jesus Christ" (Phil. 1:6). The Ultimate Survivor isn't an overcomer by being content with the status quo, but instead is motivated with a bright hope and expectation like Paul was. "I press toward the goal for the prize of the upward call of God in Christ Jesus" (Phil. 3:14).

Here's a good question for us: How are we filled with the fullness of God? There are many things vital to our growing in the Lord, like prayer, Bible study, fellowship, supporting missions, and outreach to the hungry and homeless. Is there something in particular about any of these, or is there one way that's certain to bring about our being filled with the fullness of God? This "one way" was the focus of Paul's prayer for the "saints" at Ephesus:

> That Christ may dwell in your hearts through faith;
> that you, being rooted and grounded in love, may be
> able to comprehend with all the saints what is the
> width and length and depth and height—to know
> the love of Christ which [surpasses] knowledge; that
> you may be filled with all the fullness of God.
> —EPHESIANS 3:17–19

Whatever our activities or ministries, it's a relationship with Jesus Christ experiencing the richness of His love that fills us with all the fullness of God. "Knowledge puffs up, but love edifies" (1 Cor. 8:1). Knowledge can be gained without relationship, but love only comes through relationship!

So once again we see relationship is the heart of the gospel message. We can have a variety of worthwhile goals in our Christian walk, but which goals are most pleasing to our Father?

Thus says the Lord: "Let not the wise man glory in his wisdom, Let not the mighty man glory in his might, Nor let the rich man glory in his riches; But let him who glories glory in this, That he understands and knows Me, That I am the Lord, exercising lovingkindness, [justice], and righteousness in earth. For in these I delight," says the Lord.

—Jeremiah 9:23–24

We experience what our Lord is really like when we submit to His pruning; that's when we are being "exercised" by His wonderful "loving-kindness, justice, and righteousness." When we are delighting in these things that He delights in, our *Old* nature is being replaced with the *New*, which is just more of the nature of Jesus so that we understand Him better and know Him more fully.

The Most Important Prayer

Our goal is brought into sharp focus when we listen to the most important prayer Jesus prayed on this earth:

I do not pray for these alone, but also for those who will believe in Me through their word; that they all may be one, as You, Father, are in Me, and I in You; that they also may be one in Us, that the world may believe that You sent Me. And the glory which You gave Me I have given them, that they may be one just as We are one: I in them, and You in Me; that they may be made [complete] in one, and that the world may know that You have sent Me, and have loved them as You have loved Me.

—John 17:20–23

Now, it has become abundantly clear why all the things we've been talking about have been pointing us to Jesus Christ as The Love Connection. He is where all things will be properly connected so that we can "be made complete in one." When we lose our soul for His sake, here is where we will find it. Also, this is where we will see "conformed to the image of His Son" (Rom. 8:29), "filled with all the fullness of God" (Eph. 3:19), and "put on the new man" (Eph. 4:24) are finally finished so that we can be "[complete] and [entire], lacking nothing" (James 1:4). Jesus, the most important connection in the whole universe, is revealing this mystery of God's will: "That in the dispensation of the fullness of the times He might gather together in one all things in Christ, both which are in heaven and which are on earth—in Him" (Eph. 1:10).

We can see why the word "one" conveys the idea of unity and is considered by many to be the key to the church's becoming all that God has called her to be. Ultimate Survivors confront the trials at hand, while always looking beyond to the vision and goal of *"One."* "Blessed is the man whose strength is in You, Whose heart is set on pilgrimage" (Ps. 84:5).

Most significant for us is that we finally have the best picture of where we're headed: it's that closest of love relationships on this earth that God is always drawing us into. *One* is the ultimate objective of The Challenge—it completes The Love Connection. It is the sure means of surviving life's most difficult trials. It's the ultimate cure for loneliness, and it fulfills our highest calling. "For in Him dwells all the fullness of the Godhead bodily: and you are [made full] in Him who is the head of all [rule] and [authority]" (Col. 2:9–10).

Oneness was a high priority for Paul:

Fulfill my joy by being like-minded, having the same love, [having unity of soul], of one mind.

—Philippians 2:2

I, therefore, the prisoner of the Lord, beseech you to walk worthy of the calling with which you were called, with all lowliness and gentleness, with long-suffering, bearing with one another in love, endeavoring to keep the unity of the Spirit in the bond of peace. There is one body and one Spirit, just as you were called in one hope of your calling; one Lord, one faith, one baptism; one God and Father of all, who is above all, and through all, and in you all.

—Ephesians 4:1–6

Let's remember Jesus was a model teacher. He didn't just tell others what to do, but He actually practiced the things He taught. So how did He teach the disciples to pray?

Our Father in heaven, Hallowed be Your name. Your kingdom come. Your will be done On earth as it is in heaven.

—Matthew 6:9–10

If Jesus was praying like He taught His disciples to pray, wouldn't He be praying for the kingdom to come? Could it be He prayed for *Oneness* because it's the most direct, effective way of preparing for our Father's kingdom to come and His will to be done?

The Attitude of *Oneness*

Pause for a minute or two to carefully consider this question: If the right attitude and actions were able to make us all *One*, what would they look like?

Now, let's return to the Vine Talk for a moment to consider a possibility. There we see explained the process of change—the laying down of our soul for our friends. In other places this is described as "chastening" and "various trials," yet most noteworthy to us is that Jesus calls it being a *"servant."* This very well emphasizes the radical difference of this special kind of loving, one that loves others to the extent of laying down our very soul for them:

> But Jesus called them to Himself and said, "You know that the rulers of the Gentiles lord it over them, and those who are great exercise authority over them. Yet it shall not be so among you; but whoever desires to become great among you, let him be your servant. And whoever desires to be first among you, let him be your slave—just as the Son of Man did not come to be served, but to serve, and to give His [soul] a ransom for many."
>
> —MATTHEW 20:25–28

When we are following the example of Jesus by being a *servant* we are motivated by love, not by material gain or the praise of man like a typical, hired servant might be. So our *serving* is intended to edify others, which means we are acting for their very best interests. Is there any other attitude that could truly unify all of us?

Regardless, this is the hardest thing to do in the sense that it diametrically opposes the *Old* that wants to put our interests and concerns above everybody else's. But this is the new commandment Jesus gave us; it goes beyond "love your neighbor as yourself" (Matt. 22:39). He asks us to love others "as I have loved you" (John 13:34).

To keep things in the right perspective, we must remember we didn't choose to be born with the *Old*, but we can choose to oppose it and to lose it. That choice may not be so easy when we consider that there isn't any greater love than the love that's required to do this. Yet that's a small price to pay for having an attitude that can eventually complete The Love Connection and put us in the best place of all places to be.

> For I consider that the sufferings of this present time are not worthy to be compared with the glory which shall be revealed in us.
>
> —ROMANS 8:18

"Now, wait a minute. Aren't there some other ways to go about this thing? You're telling me we all have to be *servants*? Really? Aren't there some other attitudes that can get the job done?"

Yes, but if they really can "get the job done," they will eventually take us to the attitude of a *servant*.

"But, what about if we all would just be sure to give God all the glory, or if we all would just be totally obedient to Him, don't you think that would make us *One*?"

These are worthy goals; yet, no matter how strong our determination is in such attempts it's through replacing the *Old* traits with the *New* that we are made *One* because the *Old* always resists glorifying and obeying God. But, thanks be to God; we overcome the world, the flesh, and the devil when our soul is laid down for God and our friends—and that requires the attitude and actions of a *servant*!

The *Old* traits that are replaced are traits that hinder a closer relationship with Christ, which means they are also actively resisting the coming of our Father's kingdom and His will being done. We gain the victory, however, when we gladly embrace each pruning opportunity. *One* is the picture of where we wish eventually to land because it is that closest relationship in this world that God is always drawing us toward. So *One* is our goal, and *serving* is the way that finally takes us to the place of being all that God has planned for us to be.

When Helen, my wife to be, was being baptized in her church on an Easter Sunday morning, she prayed for a man who would walk with her in following God. That night we met for the first time; about a year and a half later we were married. I have fond memories of our wedding. Pastor Tom tied the knot and Helen was stunningly beautiful.

There were other special aspects to the occasion, like the two non-traditional songs we selected, "I'll Walk with God" from the MGM movie *Student Prince* and "Climb Every Mountain" from the 1959 Rodgers and Hammerstein musical *The Sound of Music*. We now realize these were actually excellent choices for two young people who had no idea of what was ahead for them except that God had put within them some kind of a dream of being *One* with Him as well as being *One* with each other.

However, *Oneness*, which is so precious to God, is not a cake walk. We must be willing to climb every mountain that gets in the way, and ford every stream that would keep us from this dream-vision. Without it, we would perish, Yet, it needs all the love we can give, every day that we live until Christ returns—and our dream becomes reality.

Chapter 5

THE QUESTION

THE MOST POWERFUL LIFE CHANGER

Some of us can be pretty "spiritual" as long as it's "just Jesus and me" and we don't have to relate with others. Regardless, most of the shaping and molding for becoming *One* takes place with people within the body of Christ. These come from the fact that when we are born again we are instantly transferred into the kingdom of the Son of His love, the body of Christ, where we are introduced into a new way of interacting with others. What is it about relationships with others, in our marriages, or in the body of Christ that takes "all the love we can give" to bring harmony and unity?

In submitting to Christ's lordship and wanting to *serve* others in the most helpful way we can, it is good to ask them, "What is your greatest need?" But isn't their need also what we really need? Recently I saw a politician being interviewed on TV. He was asked why our political leaders can't seem to agree on solutions to our country's greatest needs. He wisely answered in words to this effect: "Until political leaders can acknowledge the real cause and seriousness of a problem, all good solutions will be rejected and ridiculed as being extreme and unnecessary."

This is the same reaction Jesus encountered with spiritual leaders after He had healed a man of blindness.

> And Jesus said, "For judgment I have come into this world, that those who do not see may see, and that those who see may be made blind." Then some of the Pharisees who were with Him heard these words, and said to Him, "Are we blind also?" Jesus said to them, "If you were blind, you would have no sin; but now you say, 'We see.' Therefore your sin remains."
>
> —JOHN 9:39–41

The Pharisees' spiritual blindness remained their greatest problem because they did not acknowledge the real nature and seriousness of their greatest need. I was once being interviewed at a small local radio station in preparation for a live on-the-air interview about counseling. After some introductory chit-chat, the young man doing the interview asked, "What is most important in having good communication between a husband and wife?"

I answered, "Forgiveness." He appeared to be both stunned and perplexed as he then repeated several times, "Forgiveness," while I nodded yes and looked for an opening to explain why. The chance never came as he then turned to making random comments on counseling. But he seemed uninterested in continuing, so our interview wound down in short order, having never really gotten off the ground. Could it be there was a problem with forgiveness in his marriage?

There are helpful books and good techniques available today for improving our communication skills. Even so, no matter how elaborate our rules and guidelines for good communications, if we are not willing to forgive, we won't be very concerned for the other person's needs, nor will we be inclined to give their ideas the same consideration that we expect for ours. So the bottom line for good communication is forgiveness. But what if the need to be forgiven was at the root of most of our problems?

Actually, confessing faults and receiving forgiveness is a vital necessity for all who are growing in Christ Jesus and wish to be a good *servant*. Remember, our need to confess began for all of us at birth because we all inherited a nature that was independent from God. Through no choice or fault of our own, we began life dominated by this nature that resisted God.

Our current problems, however, stem from the fact that whether we have been subtle or quite obvious, we all have allowed the *Old* to still have a residence in us after we committed our lives to Christ at salvation. We've made choices to save some of the *Old* rather than lose it for the sake of Christ: "For all have sinned and fall short of the glory of God" (Rom. 3:23). In His mercy and desire to draw us closer, He reveals this to us in deeper layers as we are able to handle it—it's the "peeling the onion" process.

> I still have many things to say to you, but you cannot bear them now. However, when He, the Spirit of truth, has come, He will guide you into all truth; for He will not speak on His own authority, but whatever He hears He will speak.
> —John 16:12–13

When our shortcomings are revealed, we need to ask to be forgiven. Some may say, "Sure, we all need forgiveness to be born again; but then we're a new creation and all things have become *New*. We don't need forgiveness anymore." Let's take a look at what Paul was talking about when he said, "All things have become new." First of all, let's remember Paul wrote this letter, "To the church of God which is at Corinth, with all the saints who are in all Achaia" (2 Cor. 1:1). The point is He's earnestly pleading with believers to come into something beyond salvation.

> Therefore, if anyone is in Christ, he is a new creation; old things have passed away; behold, all things have become new. Now all things are of God, who has reconciled us to Himself through Jesus Christ, and has given us the ministry of reconciliation, that is, that God was in Christ reconciling the world to Himself, not imputing their trespasses to them, and has committed to us the word of reconciliation. Now then, we are ambassadors for Christ, as though God were pleading through us: we implore you on Christ's behalf, be reconciled to God. For He made Him who knew no sin to be sin for us, that we might become the righteousness of God in Him.
>
> —2 CORINTHIANS 5:17–21

When someone is born again they have not yet been completed, but all things are new for them in the sense that they are now in a "brand new ball game." We and the angels rejoice when that happens—a soul has been saved! The devil and his cohorts fought to prevent that, but now this soul is in a new program that follows salvation; it's called "disciplining."

Disciplining requires the restoring of the soul; or as Paul refers to it here, it's being "reconciled" to God and becoming "the righteousness of God in Him." Jesus told His disciples in The Great Commission that they should be engaged in both of these activities; the saving of souls as well as the restoring of souls through teaching them what they had been taught.

> And Jesus came and spoke to them saying, "All authority has been given to Me in heaven and on earth. Go therefore and make disciples of all the nations, baptizing them in the name of the Father and of the Son and of the Holy Spirit, teaching them to observe all things that I have commanded you; and lo, I am with you always, even to the end of the age." Amen.
> —Matthew 28:18–20

If our goal in *serving* others is to take to heaven with us as many as we can, then we'll want to be sure they are being disciplined well so the enemy can't simply pick them off while they're still on the way. OK, that's a good idea. But what about forgiveness; how important is it in the process?

The Forever-Uniqueness of the Love of Christ

With the issue of forgiveness in mind, we continue our probing and exploring the goal of becoming *One* until we arrive deep at its center where we are confronted by a question that's been waiting for us there. But then, we discover it's also the same question that lives at the very heart of The Challenge, and it's there today and every day: "What am I doing with the love of Christ?"

This captivating question deserves our careful consideration. It seems to assume that everyone is doing something with the love of Christ. Yet "The Question" is unmistakably pointed at you and me; it wants us to ask ourself, "What am I doing with the love of Christ?"

It turns out that how we answer The Question is crucial to our being made *One!* It's because of the forever-uniqueness of the love of Christ—the source and fountain of all true forgiveness. Forgiveness is what powers the process of our becoming *One*, from the beginning at salvation, through the pruning, to being filled with the fullness of God. It brings us the joy of the Lord, releases us from the prisons of our fears and addictions, brings light and clarity to our minds, enlarges our capacity to forgive others, removes barriers to love relationships, and gives us the righteous boldness to walk right into the very presence of our Father.

The death of Jesus Christ through the spilling of His blood on a cross was horrendous in every way. Yet the eternal uniqueness of His sacrifice was the amount of love, beyond any measuring, that was needed in this laying down of His soul as total payment for all the sins of the whole world. He made available to the world the only complete, thoroughgoing forgiveness. If we accept it, it pays for all the sins we've ever made or ever will make. It's always effective because the old chorus about the blood of Jesus is eternally true, it'll never lose its power!

So, we are brought to this conclusion: the most powerful, life changing aspect of love is forgiveness. For this reason, it's the single, most important thing we'll ever receive, and it's the most important thing we can pass on to others.

> So Jesus said to them again. "Peace to you! As the Father has sent Me, I also send you." And when He had said this, He breathed on them, and said to them, "Receive the Holy Spirit. If you forgive the

sins of any, they [have been] forgiven them; if you
retain the sins of any, they [have been] retained."

—John 20:21–23

By a God-ordained arrangement, a marvelous blessing is
ours in this forgiveness available through the love of Christ.
The more extensive the forgiveness we receive, the more love
we have to give. Jesus illustrated this remarkable truth for
us in His visit to the home of Simon the Pharisee. In his
own reasoning, Simon doubted Christ's authority because
He was allowing a sinful woman to touch Him.

> And Jesus answered and said to him, "Simon, I
> have something to say to you." So he said, "Teacher,
> say it." "There was a certain creditor who had two
> debtors. One owed five hundred denarii, and the
> other fifty. And when they had nothing with
> which to repay, he freely forgave them both. Tell
> Me, therefore, which of them will love him more?"
> Simon answered and said, "I suppose the one whom
> he forgave more." And He said to him, "You have
> rightly judged." Then He turned to the woman and
> said to Simon, "Do you see this woman? I entered
> your house; you gave Me no water for My feet, but
> she has washed My feet with her tears and wiped
> them with the hair of her head. You gave Me no
> kiss, but this woman has not ceased to kiss My feet
> since the time I came in. You did not anoint My
> head with oil, but this woman has anointed My
> feet with fragrant oil. Therefore I say to you, her
> sins, which are many, are forgiven, for she loved
> much. But to whom little is forgiven, the same
> loves little."

—Luke 7:40–47

Then, there's a lady I know who had been struggling for a long time trying to forgive her ex-husband. She finally cried out to God, desperately asking for help. Very shortly after that, she said God began showing her things in her own life for which she needed to be forgiven. She accepted His assessment of her need, admitted her faults, received His forgiveness, and soon found she had more than enough love to forgive her ex. In this very desirable development in her life, wouldn't we have to say she was responding very well to the love of Christ?

As a matter of fact, answering The Question wisely is the way desirable outcomes are obtained in all the issues we've encountered in The Challenge. Consequently, seeing that The Q is worthy of our best consideration, we want our response to be very well thought out, especially by being aware of the most powerful forces shaping our response. Therefore, it behooves us to first investigate the legendary power behind the throne.

THE POWER BEHIND THE THRONE

In the days of kings and queens, oftentimes there was a person who had such influence on the king that they, rather than the king, actually ran the kingdom. Usually this person was not very conspicuous; they preferred to keep a low profile. However, before any change could be made within that kingdom, the power behind the throne had to approve or there would be no change. Such a power exists within our own personal kingdom.

Paul's experience showed evidence of this power operating in his life. He said he decided to do what's right in his "mind," that's where he delighted "in the law of God."

But "another law," less conspicuous, in his members actually determined his actions.

> I find then a law, that evil is present with me, the one who wills to do good. For I delight in the law of God according to the inward man. But I see another law in my members, warring against the law of my mind, and bringing me into captivity to the law of sin which is in my members.
>
> —ROMANS 7:21–23

In a similar fashion, we can decide in our mind to control our thoughts or our actions in a certain way. But then, why is it we'll find there's another decision arising from somewhere in our members that wars against this decision of our mind? In spite of that, our *Old* nature staunchly supports the deception of our being able to rule our personal kingdom from the throne of our mind, independent from the influence of our heart which has the capability of being woefully "deceitful." (See Jeremiah 17:9.) For this reason, God, in His loving-kindness, has prepared wisdom for us in Proverbs:

> Keep your heart with all diligence, For out of it spring the issues of life.
>
> —PROVERBS 4:23

Paul also warned the Ephesians of this problem. Evidently he thought it's possible for believers to still be walking in the ineffectiveness of their mind just like they were before they believed.

> This I say, therefore, and testify in the Lord, that you should no longer walk as the rest of the Gentiles walk, in the futility of their mind, having

their understanding darkened, being alienated
from the life of God, because of the ignorance that
is in them, because of the [hardness] of their heart.
—Ephesians 4:17–18

It's no wonder God tells us to keep our heart with all diligence; but it's definitely important to keep our mind also! How do we do that? Even when we have doubled the guard and are firmly determined to steel our mind against any "emotional" influences, the heart is still calling all the plays as the power behind the throne. Regardless of our preferences, the heart is the control center where all incoming data, both from the physical realm and the spiritual, is gathered, analyzed, and acted upon. The heart is where all of our thoughts, decisions, and actions originate. "For out of the heart proceed evil thoughts, murders, adulteries, fornications, thefts, false witness, blasphemies" (Matt. 15:19). The greatest life changing example of this relationship is clearly expressed in Paul's letter to the Romans:

If you confess with your mouth the Lord Jesus and
believe in your heart that God has raised Him from
the dead, you will be saved. For with the heart one
believes unto righteousness, and with the mouth
confession is made unto salvation.
—Romans 10:9–10

We begin to gain some understanding of our heart and mind's relationship with this thought: Is it possible the spiritual condition of our heart determines how well our mind functions? These verses should provide some insight:

He who loves his brother abides in the light, and
there is no cause for stumbling in him. But he who

hates his brother is in darkness and walks in darkness, and does not know where he is going, because the darkness has blinded his eyes.

—1 John 2:10–11

But the path of the just is like the [light], That shines ever brighter unto the perfect day. The way of the wicked is like darkness; They do not know what makes them stumble.

—Proverbs 4:18–19

Where the Q Is Answered

A young man who was an eligible bachelor really wanted to get married, but he was afraid of asking anyone to marry him. So he went to a psychiatrist who gave him advice on making a marriage proposal and told him to keep trying till he got accepted. A few weeks later, the young man returned to see the psychiatrist, looking very depressed and confused. "Hey Doc, now I really need some help! Since that talk we had, I have proposed to three different women. And what did that get me? I got slapped, kicked, and the redhead even tried to shoot me!"

Becoming a little self-defensive, the psychiatrist asks, "For heaven's sake, why was their reaction so violent? All I advised you to do was to propose with just a simple, sweet little question: 'Will you marry me? I love you with all my heart.'" "Yah, why did they have to go and get so heated up?" the young man asks. "And I even improved a little bit on your advice to show them that I'm an honest, upfront kind of guy. I asked, 'Will you marry me?' Then when I paused, they would ask, 'Do you love me with all your heart?' And then, because I'm an honest, upfront kind of guy, I said, 'My heart belongs to mama, but I love you with all my mind!'"

> And the LORD your God will circumcise your
> heart and the heart of your descendants, to love
> the LORD your God with all your heart and with
> all your soul, that you may live.
>
> —DEUTERONOMY 30:6

Certainly, God wants us to love Him with all our heart and with all our soul, which includes both the heart and mind. But the heart directs the soul—it's the rudder that steers the boat. Looking back at The Question, "What am I doing with the love of Christ?" isn't it quite reasonable to say the heart is where The Question eventually has to be answered? But how does the mind participate in the response? This is very important because if it fits in with God's plan, it results in our being totally changed for the better.

So here's the critical issue. How do we ever get to the place where we are able to love God with all our soul when its ability to love is restrained by Adam's DNA? *Serving* is the way, the same way all the other good things come about in our being completed. And Jesus told us how we can be free to love God with all our being:

> If you abide in My word, you are My disciples
> indeed. And you shall know the truth, and the
> truth shall make you free.
>
> —JOHN 8:31–32

We abide in His Word by actually living it, and that is very well summed up in loving God with all that we are and loving our neighbor as ourself. Jesus also showed us the best way to do that:

> Greater love has no one than this, than to lay down
> one's [soul] for his friends.
>
> —John 15:13

Essentially, laying down our soul is sacrificing our whole being, which is what we have described as *serving*. So, after salvation, the most important changes in our life take place through *serving*; and that's how we come to know the truth that sets us free to do what we're created for—to live in love relationship with Him and those around us.

Paul further elaborates on these words of Jesus using a dramatic picture of presenting our "bodies a living sacrifice." This, for sure, is not going along with the world's plan for being set free. However, here's the tremendous benefit that comes from *serving* rather than from conforming: As we are observing with our mind the wonderful changes taking place in our heart—like more love, joy, and peace—it renews our mind so that we are transformed with new understanding, coming from the fact that we now have firsthand proof that God's will for us is very good.

> I beseech you therefore, brethren, by the mercies
> of God, that you present your bodies a living sac-
> rifice, holy, acceptable to God, which is your rea-
> sonable service. And do not be conformed to this
> world, but be transformed by the renewing of your
> mind, that you may prove what is that good and
> acceptable and [complete] will of God.
>
> —Romans 12:1–2

When our mind is renewed in *serving*, the transformation can be remarkable. Every so often a report is given of someone suffering from depression who was encouraged to find a way to *serve* others. When they resisted focusing on their self and turned their heart's attention to *serving* others, it renewed their mind and they were set free of the depression. When we are able to *serve* like Jesus taught us in the Vine Talk, we are building the best defense against depression, because He said He was telling us these things in order "that My joy may remain in you, and that your joy may be full" (John 15:11).

After Paul's passionate urging us to *serve* (Rom. 12:1), in the verse 3 he said we ought to humble ourselves to *serve* "as God has dealt to each one a measure of faith." Then, for the rest of the chapter, he lists a number of specific ways to *serve* with that measure of faith so our mind can be renewed and we can be transformed with more freedom for *serving*. This, of course, brings us more joy.

How the Q Is Answered

The Challenge keeps The Q always before us. And this is true for anyone because the love of Jesus Christ is always being freely offered to everyone! This most valuable item in the whole universe, paid for with the blood of Christ, is still free to the likes of you and me. And it doesn't matter for even a wink of your eye how unworthy you may feel you are or how terrible your thoughts or actions may have been, God still loves you beyond anything you can think or imagine. He always offers the promise of a great future for anyone who will be open to the love of Christ.

We have seen how our answer is first decided in our heart; now let's see how our answer is being given in the context of *One*. "There is one body and one Spirit, just as you were called in one hope of your calling" (Eph. 4:4). When our heart is yielded and receptive to Christ's offer, His love is able to flow, by way of the Spirit, in and out of our heart. In this way, the *"flow"* comes from the heart of Christ directly to our heart and to the heart of each member of His body. Thus it may also be passed around, heart to heart, among the members.

This is how we *serve* in our place in His body, edifying one another by being in the *flow*, not "alienated from," but connected with "the life of God" (Eph. 4:18). Open to the *flow* is open to Christ and open to all that He can be to us through the Spirit. Consequently, we are being made complete in *One* by our giving and receiving through the *flow*. Depending upon the attitude of our heart, we are always deciding whether to be more open, more closed, or completely hardened against the *flow* of love that comes freely from Him who is the way, the truth, and the life.

Now we're ready to answer The Question. What am I doing with the love of Christ? You and I are responding to the offer of His love by the way we are handling the *flow* in every moment of our life. This decides our success in any of life's trials and whether or not we will be Ultimate Survivors!

THE GROUP I DIDN'T NEED

Something very special happened for me in that personal growth group Pastor Tom led. It was a very significant pruning opportunity. At that time I didn't think I had any need for a group like that because I "had it all together." But I thought I might pick up some tips for a few others I knew who "really needed some help." I had come to trust Tom; and in the security of his acceptance and approval, I was able to begin seeing signs of the deficiencies in my own makeup. It became very apparent that I was overly concerned about how others saw me. Also, why was it so uncomfortable to talk about my feelings for my dad? And it was particularly unsettling to see the unfolding results of my personality inventory that were beginning to show some chinks in my facade.

This began a major change in my life. I had been quite independent, not letting anyone get close to me. The image of an "all-right guy" who was friendly and outgoing was what I worked so hard to project. But I didn't let anyone know the real me, what was going on in my inner thoughts and feelings. Actually, I had stuffed most of those feelings way underground and well away from my own mind. And I deceptively told myself I had no need for anyone's acceptance, so that's what I brought to the group.

In the group there was a physics professor I saw as a "far out" intellectual type whom I'd probably never find interesting—I didn't need him. Then there were a couple of giggly college girls—I didn't need them. There was a sexually confused guy—I didn't need him. The "not too honest" young businessman and the others—I didn't need them either.

But that night after our group meeting, where we had received another part of the results of our personality inventory, we all were sitting in the usual after meeting place—an ice-cream parlor near the church. The results of my inventory were very disturbing, and I was humbled to the core. The inventory indicated that deeply buried fear was my strongest personality trait. In the depths of my fear was the feeling I didn't deserve acceptance. The picture I had nurtured of myself, being so "all together" and confident, was shattered. As I looked around at each member of this motley group I was a part of, I had an unusual, entirely new feeling—I needed them. I believe it was the first time in my life that my heart was opened to realize I needed approval and acceptance; but not because I deserved it or that I could earn it. God had brought me to a place in life where I was able to admit I really didn't deserve His acceptance or theirs; but now I was ready to receive it, and to receive it on those terms.

I told myself in my mind that I was acceptable, but my inner feelings and outward behavior had always shown I really didn't believe it. Now my heart was changing as I was opening it to the *flow* of God's love and forgiveness that was being conveyed to me through Tom and these people who I thought I didn't need. The weeks and months that followed were delightfully different. I was less fearful of things in general, I was more at ease with people showing interest in me as a person, and I was much more accepting and tolerant of others.

I remember the pleasant feelings of getting to know this new person in my life. But most important, I was more able to receive the acceptance that is there in my Father's eyes—and in the eyes of those who are close to Him.

Chapter 6

THE ANATOMY OF *ONE*

WHERE IT ALL COMES TOGETHER

How does the Bible picture this *Oneness* where the *flow* of the love of Christ is found? Perhaps the most descriptive picture is the analogy of the human body which Paul uses to explain the "work of ministry" in the body of Christ. Actually, this is "The Group" that the world doesn't think it needs. But we all have felt that way at one time or another. So let's see how the *flow* is involved in the anatomy and functioning of the body of Christ where we are made complete in *One*.

> And He Himself gave some to be apostles, some prophets, some evangelists, and some pastors and teachers, for the equipping of the saints for the work of ministry, for the [building up] of the body of Christ, till we all come to the unity of the faith and of the knowledge of the Son of God, to a [complete] man, to the measure of the stature of the fullness of Christ; that we should no longer be children, tossed to and fro and carried about with every wind of doctrine, by the trickery of men, in the cunning craftiness of deceitful plotting, but, speaking the truth in love, may grow up in all

things into Him who is the head—Christ—from
whom the whole body, joined and knit together by
what every joint supplies, according to the effective
working by which every part does its share, causes
growth of the body for the [building up] of itself
in love.
—Ephesians 4:11–16

Here we see all the things that we've been talking about
are coming together in "the work of the ministry." The
various parts of the overriding theme of "change" running
through all of our discussions now come to the desired
conclusion—"To a [complete] man, to the measure of the
stature of the fullness of Christ." This is the goal of "the
work of ministry" with all functions of the body working
together with the one purpose of "[building up] of the body
of Christ" into a closer love relationship that is ultimately
completed in *One*.

Building up, or edifying, restores us to the intention
of God's original creation. Way back then God said, "Let
Us make man in Our image, according to Our likeness"
(Gen. 1:26). So now God is doing what is truly amazing;
His desire is to restore each one of us to that "likeness" by
having provided this arrangement for us to be built up into
Christ, "for in Him dwells all the fullness of the Godhead
bodily" (Col. 2:9).

Building up into Christ is, essentially, a matter of being
filled with more of Him as our *Old* is replaced by a *New*
nature that comes from Him. Where this ultimate of
changes so often takes place, as we have frequently observed,
is in pruning opportunities. We will be making a fuller
observation of the pruning process in this context of the
anatomy as we take note of how each function fits in. In

this way we will see how important the *flow* is in doing our part most effectively.

THE HEAD

Jesus Christ is the head of the body; it's for His benefit that pruning and all other functions are intended. "All things were created through Him and for Him" (Col. 1:16). Some day every tongue will confess that Jesus Christ is Lord, and He is worthy of all honor and glory, yet in a most astonishing way He wants to share His glory with the likes of you and me! "And the glory which You gave Me I have given them, that they may be one just as We are one" (John 17:22).

The Love Connection which we have when we are rightly connected with Jesus is what connects us through Him with the Father and all of the other members. When we are accordingly "joined and knit together" through the *flow*, we can expect to be pruned as a normal part of *serving*. Each time we're pruned, we're able to *serve* more effectively. This puts us in an ongoing, upward cycle, growing more and more into the image of Christ; and thus The Love Connection is being completed.

FAITH

Drawing closer to God is what pleases Him—this is what makes faith so valuable. Without faith we could miss the pruning opportunities God wants to use to bring us more fully into His presence. On the other hand, *with* faith we will be seeking Him by welcoming those opportunities no matter how repulsive they may be to our *Old* nature; because we're expecting a reward, and there are no greater rewards than His.

> But without faith it is impossible to please Him,
> for he who comes to God must believe that He is,
> and that He is a rewarder of those who diligently
> seek Him.
>
> —HEBREWS 11:6

Here is where the most crucial battles of the cosmic conflict take place. God, with deepest longings, is always intent on bringing us closer to Him, while at the same time the devil is fiercely striving to separate us as far as possible from God. But here's the essential truth: which way the battle is going at any moment is determined by our faith. Yet, because of our Father's loving-kindness, He always allows us complete freedom to choose whether we will trust Him or not. Jesus reveals enough of the Father for us to have good reason to trust Him, but not so much that we can't rationalize our way out of trusting Him if our heart isn't in it.

The *flow* of the love of Christ carries the brightest hopes and warmest expectations that support great faith. However, the devil prods our *Old* nature as it is working, usually undercover, to energize and justify our resisting the *flow*. So we need a basic faith that opens our heart to the *flow* and keeps us properly connected. Let's think of it as a "working" faith; because as we remain in the *flow*, our understanding and knowledge of God grows, strengthening us in the unity of the faith on the way to *One*. Here is a "basic faith" that serves the purpose:

"God loves me, and He has the best plan for my life."

So what's the devil's strategy to overcome our faith? There are a couple ways he seems to use most often. First, he has found it's exceedingly easy to get us to harden our heart if he can convince us God isn't being very loving toward us when we're being pruned. Jesus warned of this possibility of being offended in a response to John the Baptist. John had sent two of his disciples to ask Jesus:

> "Are you the Coming One, or do we look for another?" Jesus answered and said to them, "Go and tell John the things which you hear and see. The blind see and the lame walk; the lepers are cleansed and the deaf hear; the dead are raised up and the poor have the gospel preached to them. And blessed is he who is not offended because of Me."
> —MATTHEW 11:3–6

In this world's reasoning, we could say things weren't going well for John at that time. Herod had put him in prison and soon after this he would have him beheaded. Understandably John had some "logical reasons" for being a bit unhappy about how things were going for him, feeling that God wasn't treating him like He should have been treated. In His compassionate reply, Jesus first assured John that he *was* in God's will, that his preparing the way for Him had not been a mistake because these signs showed He is "the Coming One."

We can be sure Jesus was deeply moved by His friend's predicament but gave no indication of being surprised or dismayed. Instead He encouraged John to endure his situation without being offended because those who are doing God's will can look forward to the joy of hearing our heavenly Father say, "Well done, good and faithful servant" (Matt. 25:21, 23). And, of course, this was what later encouraged Jesus on the cross: "Who for the joy that was set before Him endured the cross" (Heb. 12:2).

If the devil can't get us out of the joy of the Lord and

out of the *flow* by prodding us to be offended, he still has another strategy that he frequently uses. This is to accuse us of being so unworthy that we won't even think of being open to the *flow* if he can deceive us to believe that God and everybody else thinks we're not good enough. Regardless of how the enemy may be working to defeat our faith, his goal is to get us to abandon God's plan with a protest:

"I have a better plan, and I'm looking out for me."

In view of what we're up against, it would be wise for us to find a strategy that is entirely adequate to overcome the devil and his strategies. In the revelation that John had on the island of Patmos, he saw a terrific battle in heaven which ended with the devil and his angels being cast out. In his account we see listed the three parts of a successful strategy for overcoming our "accuser:" "the blood of the Lamb," "the word of their testimony," and "their souls."

> Then I heard a loud voice saying in heaven, "Now salvation, and strength, and the kingdom of our God, and the power of His Christ have come, for the accuser of our brethren, who accused them before our God day and night, has been cast down. And they overcame him by the blood of the Lamb and by the word of their testimony, and they did not love their [souls] to the death"
> —REVELATION 12:10–11

The blood of the Lamb

We may not be too surprised when the enemy brings us accusations through those who don't like us, but what may catch us off guard are false accusations that come from those we respect and who we thought liked us. Also, one of his clever tricks is to bring them directly to us as harassing thoughts, which he tries to make look like our thoughts, something we came up with on our own. Regardless, our response as a faithful, overcoming *servant* will always be to first ask God to show us if the accusations are valid. If God shows us we are at fault, we need to admit our sin, ask to be forgiven, accept the blood of Christ as full payment for our sin, and make appropriate amends. Of course, this may entail some real crucifying of the flesh; but it's always worth the price to keep the *flow* of love open between us and God.

> Now no [disciplining] seems to be joyful for the present, but painful; nevertheless, afterward it yields the peaceable fruit of righteousness to those who have been trained by it.
> —HEBREWS 12:11

On the other hand, if our conduct has been in keeping with the Word of God and our heart doesn't condemn us when we're asking God for His guidance, then we can walk on in confidence, knowing that His approval has far greater weight than the disapproval of hundreds of accusers.

The word of their testimony

In his attempts to separate us from our Father, the devil often accuses us of foolishly trusting in God, especially when it looks like He may have forgotten about us or He's asking us to do what seems too difficult or maybe impossible. At these times it can be very helpful to remember our "testimony." Here testimony is used with the meaning of "evidence obtained through personal experience." So we overcome the enemy and his accusations by reminding ourself, and others if appropriate, of past experiences when we trusted God in spite of the overwhelming odds against us and He victoriously brought us through.

An exciting example of this is seen in the account of

David's killing Goliath. People were telling him he was too small to go out to face this giant Philistine; but David, who seemed to be unfazed by the warnings, must have gained strong confidence in God through his experiences of trusting Him in the past. "Moreover David said, 'The LORD, who delivered me from the paw of the lion and from the paw of the bear, He will deliver me from the hand of the Philistine.' And Saul said to David, 'Go, and the LORD be with you!'" (1 Sam. 17:37).

Cliff Hanger Reviews are what we have had many times in our family when it has seemed like we were hanging on the edge of a cliff about to go over the edge if the events, sometimes seemingly impossible, didn't unfold the way we needed them to. I remember the first one of these conferences that took place early one morning before time to get up. Helen and I gathered the kids, who were quite young at the time, and crowded them together with us in our bed. The kids really liked this cozy, get-together idea, but all of us were really very concerned about the ramifications of a major move across the country if I was accepted for an unusually interesting chaplain's position the Lord appeared to be leading me to.

Sure, our faith had been tested before; nevertheless, in this one the uncertainties and risks were far more scary. What we did then became a simple pattern which we have often followed as a way to overcome the accuser's attempts to get us to discard our faith. With everyone's help, we recalled and reviewed those times before when God took us through other chancy situations where we were endeavoring to walk in His will. This "review" encouraged us and the move did take place with good results. However, let's not miss the best part of this picture; just like with David and our other brothers and sisters in the Lord, the challenges get bigger—but our testimony and faith will continue to grow stronger if we stand firm, trusting Him!

Their soul

We can obtain complete assurance of forgiveness and have a powerful testimony when we are accused; yet the thing that finally allows us to overcome any attempt of the devil to take us down is our willingness to put to death any part of our *Old* nature that God asks us to. With that state of mind, we can know the deepest satisfaction and optimum joy and discover how God's loving-kindness is much more valuable than life itself.

> Because Your lovingkindness is better than life, My lips shall praise You. Thus I will bless You while I live; I will lift up my hands in Your name. My soul shall be satisfied as with marrow and fatness, And my mouth shall praise You with joyful lips.
> —PSALM 63:3–5

One of our mightiest weapons in resisting the enemy and his strategy is in exulting God through our thanksgiving and praise. That directly counteracts the devil's efforts to separate us from God's love by opening our hearts wider to the *flow*. This is laying down our soul for our best friend, Jesus Christ, by crucifying the flesh which wants to glory self. Although this is rightly called a sacrifice, it's clearly for our benefit.

> Therefore by Him let us continually offer the sacrifice of praise to God, that is, the fruit of our lips, giving thanks to His name.
> —HEBREWS 13:15

> In everything give thanks; for this is the will of
> God in Christ Jesus for you.
>
> —1 THESSALONIANS 5:18

Furthermore, this reinforces our overcoming with a more imposing presence of God as He inhabits our praises. "But You are holy, Enthroned in the praises of Israel" (Ps. 22:3). This is an indispensable part of our knowing the awesome intimacy of The Love Connection. Remember, it's this intimacy, being rightly related with God and those around us, that empowers us to overcome all of the enemy's temptations—like illicit sexual relations, pornography, drugs, addictions, or lust for political or financial power. These have no appeal for us when the deepest needs for the right kind of intimacy and desires of our heart are being satisfied in God's plan for our life—that eliminates the pain of loneliness!

> Trust in the LORD, and do good; Dwell in the land,
> and feed on His faithfulness. Delight yourself also
> in the LORD, And He shall give you the desires of
> your heart.
>
> —PSALM 37:3–4

IN LOVE

The power that makes possible the deepest kind of beneficial change is found in the love of Christ. This is what strengthens us to deny the old Self-serving and put on the trait of God-serving so we can endure the pruning and willingly *serve* others. So it's not too surprising that we find we are making the best use of pruning opportunities when we are open to the *flow*, and here's how it happens:

These opportunities come when we are resisting doing

what we know is right and good; we are hanging on to some part of the *Old*. But if we remain in the *flow*, the Holy Spirit's presence can make us so uncomfortable with our resisting Him that the situation turns into a pruning opportunity, which we can accept or which we might try to avoid by quickly closing our heart to the *flow*.

By remaining in the *flow*, however, we have present with us whatever is needed for the pruning process. By abiding in His love, we can be secure enough to admit our need for correction and to ask Him to forgive us. We then humbly accept His forgiveness. This most powerful life-changing aspect of love is freely given—but it's given to be accepted on His terms: First, we don't deserve it because we haven't earned it, nor is there any way for us to earn it—it's a gift. Secondly, we accept the sacrifice of His Son as full payment for our sin, no matter what the sin is.

Fully accepting His forgiveness means we have now let go of something in our *Old* nature and we are taking on the part of His nature He's offering us so that we are built up more fully into Him.

There's no need to ask, "Can I love myself," or "Can I forgive myself?" The big question is, "Can I accept Christ's forgiveness and love for me on His terms?" Remember, it's the depth of our confession that determines the depth of our forgiveness, and the depth of our forgiveness determines the depth of the joy we receive and the depth of the love we will have to give.

Let's consider some situations where we may need forgiveness. It is definitely needed when we are less open to receiving the *flow*. This attitude may be due to our being angry with God; He hasn't answered our prayers or we feel He's being unkind to us. Being open and honest enough to tell God how we feel pleases Him, just as it pleases any good father. Nevertheless, if we also need to ask Him for understanding as to how He wants to use these circumstances to bring us into more of His nature, be thankful that He's open and patient with us. Remember, we are the one who needs to change—He's always right and good.

Also, we may be less open to receive if we feel we are not worthy to receive. Whatever the reason for our feeling unworthy, we should ask God to forgive us and accept His forgiveness, which is freely offered for all sin or feelings of unworthiness if we only admit our guilt. When we accept His forgiveness, we are acting on our believing "God loves me, and He has the best plan for my life." But if we are still restricting the *flow* of His love into our heart, whether directly from God or through others, we are saying His plan isn't adequate; "I have a better plan, and I'm looking out for me."

Someone may say, "I believe God can forgive me—but I'm the one who is still not able to forgive me." There could be several possibilities for this. One possibility could be that we are still foolishly trying to earn our own forgiveness. We might be thinking: *His conditions for forgiveness are nice, but I'm going to make mine more effective because I'm making mine more demanding.* But that just doesn't work: "Who can say, 'I have made my heart clean, I am pure from my sin'?" (Prov. 20:9).

Another possibility is there's a lingering remnant of guilt if we haven't brought all of the guilt out into the light so it can be forgiven.

And, of course, another is that the devil, "the accuser of our brethren," may be making some progress in falsely accusing us of not being forgiven. A good remedy for that is to confess our faults to a trustworthy Christian friend who can forgive us on Christ's behalf and then stand with us as a witness to our forgiveness when it's needed to disprove the enemy's lies. (See James 5:16; John 20:23; Matt. 18:16.)

Perhaps the most difficult time for recognizing our need to be forgiven is when we have closed off the *flow* because of anger. When we act in our *Old* nature with anger, we have closed the *flow*. It's not possible to be open to the *flow* while at the same time being out of the *flow*, acting with anger. Yet our *Old* nature is very capable of so justifying our fleshly anger that it's easy to ignore our being closed to God's love at that time.

In short, what qualifies us for forgiveness are simply two conditions: contrite and humble. When confronted by a pruning opportunity, a contrite spirit acknowledges the need to be forgiven and the continuing possibility of that need right up till the day of Christ. Then, once we've acknowledged our need, a humble spirit will enable us to abandon our prideful plans to make ourself righteous, accept God's solution, and we are forgiven.

> For thus says the High and Lofty One Who inhabits eternity, whose name is Holy: "I dwell in the high and holy place, with him who has a contrite and humble spirit, To revive the spirit of the humble, And to revive the heart of the contrite ones."
> —Isaiah 57:15

Above all, we never need to be troubled with a feeling of being unworthy because of the forever-uniqueness of the love of Christ—the power of His blood to cover all sin and unworthiness! The more diligent we are to be walking in forgiveness, the more forgiveness we will be able to give to those around us who are so in need of this special expression of the love of Christ. And let us be quick to forgive, for Jesus said:

> If you forgive men their trespasses, your heavenly Father will also forgive you. But if you do not forgive men their trespasses, neither will your Father forgive your trespasses.
>
> —MATTHEW 6:14–15

EVERY PART

It's vital that we are giving and receiving the *flow* in all of our relations with other parts of the body because "every part" has the potential to contribute significantly to every other part's growth and spiritual well-being. This comes not only from the ministry and gifts of the Holy Spirit, but from the primary fact that we are receiving Christ when we receive our brothers and sisters in the Lord. Whether they are someone we think to be "important," or just a plain ol' "righteous man," we are receiving the Lord and we will be rewarded for doing so. Jesus promised:

> He who receives you receives Me, and he who receives Me receives Him who sent Me. He who receives a prophet in the name of a prophet shall receive a prophet's reward. And he who receives a righteous man in the name of a righteous man shall receive a righteous man's reward. And whoever gives one of these little ones only a cup of cold water in the name of a disciple, assuredly, I say to you, he shall by no means lose his reward.
>
> —MATTHEW 10:40–42

For some of us, what we're talking about may be the most difficult aspect of *serving*; and yet it's one of the most important ways of edifying others while being edified ourself. It's acknowledging the worth and validity of someone else's part in the body. When we're receiving their ministry, we are receiving them and the One who sent them. In this way, we are acknowledging the truth that both they and we are valuable, genuine parts of the body of Christ.

Jesus laid it out to Peter. "Peter said to Him, 'You shall never wash my feet!' Jesus answered him, 'If I do not wash you, you have no part with Me'" (John 13:8).

A most excellent test for our level of maturity and completeness is how well we do in "submitting to one another in the fear of God" (Eph. 5:21). It's easy to say, "I love God with all my heart"; but for most of us, the proof of our love is seen in how well we are able to submit to others. This submission to others is kept appropriate if it is truly done "in the fear of God," because we are ultimately accountable to God. We fear displeasing Him above all others because He is our first love. There are a number of ways that this tests our growth in the Lord:

+ It shows whether we fear God or man, whether we are *serving* self or God.

+ It reveals how loving and obedient we are by our willingness to lay down our soul for our friends.

+ It indicates the level of our security in the Lord and our sense of personal worth.

◆ It demonstrates the strength of our basic faith and our willingness to be changed into His likeness.

Also, here are a couple of useful guidelines for this vital matter of submitting. For one, it's important to be open to each other. "But if we walk in the light as He is in the light, we have fellowship with one another, and the blood of Jesus Christ His Son cleanses us from all sin" (1 John 1:7). Our *Old* nature doesn't like the light; it flees from the light, abandoning strongholds where it was hiding to avoid close relationship. In this way more room is made for our *New* nature which, by contrast, desires to know and be known.

The other is the Golden Rule. "Therefore, whatever you want men to do to you, do also to them for this is the Law and the Prophets" (Matt. 7:12). When someone is *serving* us through speaking the truth in love, for example, we receive them like we would want them to receive us. So we diligently listen, consider, and objectively test their input, being ultimately accountable to God, so that we can then "hold fast what is good" (1 Thess. 5:21).

When submitting entails sacrificing any of our *Old* traits, we need to remember it's just part of the basic routine that shapes us for the unique place in the body of Christ where we can be all that God has planned for us to be. It's where we bring Him the greatest glory and where we find our greatest joy.

A church had a charming gazebo on its property where members would occasionally gather for special, small-scale events or just informal get-togethers. A decision was made to build a large fireplace in the center of this open-sided structure. Church members eagerly pitched in to do the job. Native stones with a variety of shapes and colors had been gathered from the surrounding area by the men in the church and were in a huge pile near the spot selected for the fireplace. One of the men was a skilled mason who was cementing the stones together to form what would become a truly beautiful fireplace.

He would pick up a stone from the pile, look it over as he turned it in his hand, and then begin hacking and shaping it with his trowel. Next, he would apply some cement and then position it exactly as he had intended in the right relationship with the other stones in the place he had prepared for it. Every so often after he had struck a stone only a few times, he would throw it into the reject pile. A young man asked him, "Why did you reject that stone?" The mason said, "It's not a living stone." A living stone is not easily offended, so it can submit to being shaped and formed without totally falling apart.

> Coming to Him as to a living stone, rejected indeed by men, but chosen by God and precious, you also, as living stones, are being built up a spiritual house, a holy priesthood, to offer up spiritual sacrifices acceptable to God through Jesus Christ.
>
> —1 PETER 2:4–5

FROM WHOM

Overall, the anatomy with all its functions expresses law and order under the unmistakable authority of Christ "from whom" the whole body is directed through the *flow*. When we're talking about being under the authority of Christ, we are entertaining the most serious threats to the roots of the *Old* nature, the trait of Self-serving. That's because "from whom" we are taking directions shows whom we are *serving*.

Let's look at some reasons why this trait must be dealt with head on.

Self-serving not only keeps us from having the satisfaction of helping to make positive changes in the lives of others, it also robs us of the joy of good fellowship with others. Worst of all is the devastating possibility of missing out on truly knowing the One who created us for His pleasure. But it is out of consideration for both His pleasure and ours that Jesus warns us of the serious consequences of Self-serving. He told of how He will rebuke some folks on "that day" for ministering apart from relationship with Him, even though they will claim they had ministered in His name.

> Not everyone who says to Me "Lord, Lord," shall enter the kingdom of heaven, but he who does the will of My Father in heaven. Many will say to Me in that day "Lord, Lord, have we not prophesied in Your name, cast out demons in Your name, and done many wonders in Your name?" And then I will declare to them, "I never knew you; depart from Me, you who practiced lawlessness!"
> —MATTHEW 7:21–23

How do we make sure this doesn't happen to us? Then, perhaps, it's good to ask, "From whom am I taking directions; or under what authority am I serving?" The "lawless" ones in this account, apparently, are Self-serving. They are under their own authority, doing things that Christians do but not really *serving* as someone who is actually acknowledging Jesus as Lord. Also, we know that authentic *serving* may involve "taking authority," for example, over evil principalities. So let's look to our model, Jesus Christ, to see how He handled authority.

> Now when He came into the temple, the chief
> priests and the elders of the people confronted
> Him as He was teaching, and said, "By what
> authority are You doing these things? And who
> gave You this authority?"
>
> —Matthew 21:23

Jesus didn't answer their question because they refused
to answer a question He gave them, which would have
given them a better understanding of authority. This
encounter was in sharp contrast, however, to the way He
was approached by someone who understood authority and
clearly recognized His authority. That's when Jesus was
greatly impressed.

> Now when Jesus had entered Capernaum, a cen-
> turion came to Him, pleading with Him, saying,
> "Lord, my servant is lying at home paralyzed,
> dreadfully tormented." And Jesus said to him, "I
> will come and heal him." The centurion answered
> and said, "Lord, I am not worthy that You should
> come under my roof. But only speak a word, and
> my servant will be healed. For I also am a man
> under authority, having soldiers under me. And I
> say to this one, 'Go,' and he goes; and to another,
> 'Come,' and he comes; and to my servant, 'Do this,'
> and he does it." When Jesus heard it, He marveled,
> and said to those who followed, "Assuredly, I say to
> you, I have not found such great faith, not even in
> Israel! And I say to you that many will come from
> east and west, and sit down with Abraham, Isaac,
> and Jacob in the kingdom of heaven. But the sons
> of the kingdom will be cast out into outer darkness.
> There will be weeping and gnashing of teeth." Then
> Jesus said to the centurion, "Go your way; and as

you have believed, so let it be done for you." And
his servant was healed that same hour.

—MATTHEW 8:5–13

There will be many coming from far and wide who will
enter the kingdom, but some, even "sons of the kingdom,"
will not recognize or accept Jesus Christ's authority and will
be "cast out into outer darkness." So the faith that made
such a strong impression on Jesus was the Centurion's belief
that Jesus was "under authority." Jesus hadn't seen that kind
of faith anywhere else in Israel, not even in the chief priests
and elders, the ones who should be experts in recognizing
God's authority. The incident demonstrated this truth: One
who has authority is under authority.

And as our model for *serving*, Jesus was always under
authority. So wouldn't it be wise for us to make certain we
are always under authority? Let's see how Jesus described
His being under authority. It's obvious He was definitely
not Self-serving, but He was God-serving as He diligently
followed His Father's directions, even to the extent of only
doing and saying what had been given to Him by the Father.
He flatly admitted He could do nothing apart from His
Father.

> For I have come down from heaven, not to do My
> own will, but the will of Him who sent Me.
>
> —JOHN 6:38

> Then Jesus answered and said to them, "Most
> assuredly, I say to you, the Son can do nothing of
> Himself, but what He sees the Father do; for what-
> ever He does, the Son also does in like manner."
>
> —JOHN 5:19

> For I have not spoken [from Myself]; but the
> Father who sent Me gave Me a command, what I
> should say and what I should speak.
>
> —John 12:49

These are sons of God

We know it's good that we aspire to be like Jesus. He is our best example in everything, especially in our learning to be under authority, even though His example may seem completely beyond our reach. Regardless, each of us should feel strongly encouraged to exercise whatever measure of faith we have to do our Father's will. But if we're not at this time seeing or hearing exact directions like Jesus did, how do we *serve* under His authority?

The final authority for all of our *serving* is the Word of God, the Holy Bible. All of our directions, and in whatever ways we are being led, are valid when they are in agreement with the Word which was given "that the man of God may be [fitted], thoroughly equipped for every good work" (2 Tim. 3:17). In applying the Word to the specifics of our life, we are led by the Holy Spirit. "For as many as are led by the Spirit of God, these are sons of God" (Rom. 8:14).

When we are open to the *flow*, we are open to the Holy Spirit and can be led by Him in a variety of ways. That's when, for example, our conscience is more sensitive so that it can give us a feeling of what's right or wrong in a situation. We can also experience a "quickening" when reading or hearing a particular verse so that it comes alive to us in a special way that gives us direction for the matter at hand. Then there's the possibility of feeling a "check" in our spirit that cautions us against proceeding with something that would have undesirable consequences.

These can be very helpful. Yet much of our praying for

others simply arises from the compassion stirred up by the love of Christ within us. As a matter of fact, having a genuine compassion for the needs of others is an excellent test of whether we are in the Spirit or we are just motivated by some self-interest. We must always be on guard against the *Old* nature, which promotes lawlessness by consistently resisting the Holy Spirit, prodding us to exult ourselves and demonstrate our importance by ministering on our own, outside of a fellowship with God.

One important way of being more specifically led that is often mentioned in the Bible involves "rhema," which now takes us to a brief word study. Most Bible versions use the same term "word" as the English translation for two different Greek words, *logos* and *rhema*. Logos is special for the fact that Jesus is called "logos," translated "the Word." "In the beginning was the Word, and the Word was with God, and the Word was God" (John 1:1). Logos is forever and unchanging. "Heaven and earth will pass away, but My words will by no means pass away" (Matt. 24:35).

On the other hand, rhema is different in some ways which also make it quite special. It can be more personally directing and specific. But let's see how rhema is used in the Bible:

> But He answered and said, "It is written, 'Man shall not live by bread alone, but by every [rhema] that proceeds from the mouth of God.'"
> —MATTHEW 4:4

(Note: in this book, rhema enclosed in brackets indicates where the Greek text shows a form of rhema.)

Here we see that rhema from God conveys the essentials for life; that is, for the kind of life that Jesus promised. We know that one of the most important of these essentials He provides in this way is "faith" because "the just shall live by faith" (Rom. 1:17).

But how do we get faith? "So then faith comes by hearing, and hearing by the [rhema] of God" (Rom. 10:17). It's important to recognize that faith originates in God, and that we can receive it from Him in a rhema.

Furthermore, we see that rhema is fresh—it "proceeds" from the mouth of God. That's even fresher than our daily bread! And that's good news because we need it on a continuing basis, 24/7. God speaks a rhema with the same motive He has in all that He does—to show His love, drawing us into closer, more immediate fellowship with Him.

There is a wide range of ways in biblical accounts where rhema came. Sometimes it was from God directly to individuals but at other times it came from God through prophets or an angel, like when Gabriel brought Mary a rhema regarding her conceiving and bringing forth a Son. (See Luke 1:26–38.) When she asked, "How can this be?" (v. 34), Gabriel said: "For with God [not any rhema] will be impossible" (v. 37).

God's rhema can bring many beneficial essentials. Look at what came to Mary in this rhema: She received an unforgettable assurance of her acceptance and worth. "Rejoice, highly favored one, the Lord is with you; blessed are you among women" (v. 28). Direction was given and special meaning and purpose was explained for her life; "call His name JESUS" (v. 31), and, "of His kingdom there will be no end" (v. 33). She was told of things to come, "the Holy Spirit will come upon you" (v. 35). She was given an encouraging word of knowledge; "Elizabeth your relative has also conceived a son" (v. 36). The overall effect of the rhema was that it brought faith to sustain her during the difficult months and years ahead.

Rhema also facilitates closeness and helps us to avoid ministering like the "lawless" ones in Matthew 7:21–23. When we are taking authority or declaring something in the name of Jesus, we want to be acting under Christ's authority and on His behalf. But didn't the lawless ones say they had ministered in the name of Jesus? That sounds like they were doing what was right. So, what were they missing? Jesus said:

> And whatever you ask in My name, that I will do, that the Father may be glorified in the Son. If you ask anything in My name, I will do it.
>
> —JOHN 14:13–14

> If you abide in Me, and My [rhema] abide[s] in you, you will ask what you desire, and it shall be done for you.
>
> —JOHN 15:7

In John 14 Jesus encourages us to ask in His name. In the next chapter He shows us the two conditions necessary for this. First, we must abide in Him, which we do by abiding in His love. "If you keep My commandments, you will abide in My love, just as I have kept My Father's commandments and abide in His love" (John 15:10).

Secondly, we stay close to Him and welcome Him to direct us with His rhema. It's impossible to do these two things and not be more and more conformed to His image and see our desires become more like His. Therefore, we can glorify Christ more fully because we are both able and have a greater desire to act faithfully in His name.

THE PRAYER OF FAITH

Rhema can be particularly helpful in praying. When we are praying for the sick and in all of our prayers for others, it's imperative that we remember God's priorities. Namely, God certainly wants all of us to be enjoying perfect health, but our loving Father is far more concerned with the saving of our soul. "If your right eye causes you to [stumble], pluck it out and cast it from you; for it is more profitable for you that one of your members perish, than for your whole body to be cast into hell" (Matt. 5:29).

Furthermore, God's priority goal for the one being prayed for and the one praying is that they both will be brought closer to Him as a result. For these reasons, rhema can be a vital part of effective prayers. Let's see how this can happen.

> Is anyone among you sick? Let him call for the elders of the church, and let them pray over him, anointing him with oil in the name of the Lord. And the prayer of faith will save the sick, and the Lord will raise him up. And if he has committed sins, he will be forgiven. Confess your trespasses to one another, and pray for one another, that you may be healed. The effective, [supplication] of a righteous man avails much. Elijah was a man with a nature like ours, and he prayed earnestly that it would not rain; and it did not rain on the land for three years and six months. And he prayed again, and the heaven gave rain, and the earth produced its fruit.
>
> —JAMES 5:14–18

God has the best way for us to pray for any person because what's true for us is also true for them: "God loves me, and He has the best plan for my life." Consequently, when we are praying for someone, it is wise that we seek such openness to the *flow* that we are abiding in Christ and His rhema is abiding in us so we can pray a "prayer of faith," which is simply praying what God has shown or told us to pray for that person. The prayer could be a simple, "Be healed!" Or it might be elaborate and in several parts. For example, God might first wish to assure them of His love for them as a person before He goes on to deal with things separating them from Him and from their healing. Then additional prayers of binding or loosing, for example, may be called for.

The person being healed has new confidence to draw closer to God through having embraced this opportunity to "grow in the grace and knowledge of our Lord and Savior Jesus Christ" (2 Pet. 3:18). The person praying is drawn closer to God through having this opportunity to deny the *Old* nature. *Old* wants us to trust in ourself and lean on our own understanding. Our flesh likes the idea of "the tail wagging the dog." But Ultimate Survivors wisely follow God's leading.

> I will instruct you and teach you in the way you should go; I will guide you with My eye.
> —Psalm 32:8

> When You said, "Seek My face," My heart said to You, "Your face, Lord, I will seek."
> —Psalm 27:8

A true *servant* likes the idea of taking orders from "the Boss." It's the way to be sure we are doing our part in seeing that God's will is being done on earth as it is in heaven. Jesus explained this arrangement to Peter. Just like He was authorized and directed by His Father in heaven, He told Peter he too would be given authority and direction from heaven to do the things on earth which had already been done in heaven: "And I will give you the keys of the kingdom of heaven, and whatever you bind on earth will [have been] bound in heaven, and whatever you loose on earth will [have been] loosed in heaven" (Matt. 16:19).

Elijah was a man with a very human nature just like you and me. Nevertheless, God worked astounding miracles through his prayers because Elijah remained in close relationship with Him. In this way he was open to God's words, which often brought him detailed directions for what he should do and the faith to pray with extraordinary boldness.

> And Elijah the Tishbite, of the inhabitants of Gilead, said to Ahab, "As the LORD God of Israel lives, before whom I stand, there shall not be dew nor rain these years, except at my word." Then the word of the LORD came to him, saying, "Get away from here and turn eastward, and hide by the Brook Cherith, which flows into the Jordan. And it will be that you shall drink from the brook, and I have commanded the ravens to feed you there."
> —1 KINGS 17:1–4

> Then the word of the LORD came to him, saying, "Arise, go to Zarephath, which belongs to Sidon, and dwell there. See, I have commanded a widow there to provide for you."
> —1 KINGS 17:8–9

> And it came to pass after many days that the word of the LORD came to Elijah, in the third year, saying, "Go, present yourself to Ahab, and I will send rain on the earth."
> —1 KINGS 18:1

"But we don't have to have such specific direction for healings, do we? And doesn't God want everyone to be healed?"

No and yes. It's not written somewhere that we must
have specific directions to pray for someone's healing. And
sure, God would like to see everyone healed and living in
the fullness of His joy. Yet, preferring to have specific directions and seeking a rhema from God are excellent ways to
make our prayers effective like Elijah's; and this helps us
avoid being one of the "lawless" ones. We can be sure Jesus
was specifically led at all times, like at the Pool of Bethesda
when He bypassed many people who were in need of healing
as He was being led to just one particular man.

Also, it is good when godly "elders of the church," who
are open to the *flow*, gather to pray for someone. In God's
loving thoughtfulness, He's given us a special way to ensure
we are ministering "in the Spirit," in the *flow*, and in right
fellowship with Him. "For where two or three are gathered together in My name, I am there in the midst of them"
(Matt. 18:20). When we are gathered together in His name,
He is present to guide us because we're abiding in Him and
His rhema is abiding in us. So if there is prophecy, casting
out demons, or wonders being done "in His name," we can
confirm and encourage each other's ministry with the guidance each of us is receiving.

In giving us this crucial guidance, Jesus quoted from the
law given by Moses: "By the mouth of two or three witnesses every [rhema] may be established" (Matt. 18:16). This
can be applied broadly to the different aspects of our ministering. Paul, for example, applies it this way to prophecy:
"Let two or three prophets speak, and let the others [dis-
cern]" (1 Cor. 14:29). This instruction was given so that
things would be done decently and in order in the church.
But it makes no difference where the location is, it's still a

valid way to increase our confidence for ministering in the Spirit while insuring it's His will being done—not ours.

After quoting Moses for this guideline, three verses later Jesus emphasizes its importance by referring to it again, "Again I say to you," and then shows us how it applies to another situation. This is when two or three of us have gathered together in His name. Then we are under the authority of Christ and He is right there in our midst to direct us so each one is a witness to how He's directing us. When we see that the "orders from headquarters" each one is receiving are the same, or are "in agreement," we'll know we "got it right." We can then be sure we are in the Spirit, and can boldly act on those directions with confidence, "For with God [not any rhema] will be impossible" (Luke 1:37).

> By the mouth of two or three witnesses every [rhema] may be established.... Assuredly, I say to you, whatever you bind on earth will [have been] bound in heaven, and whatever you loose on earth will [have been] loosed in heaven. Again I say to you that if two of you agree on earth concerning anything that they ask, it will [happen] for them [from] My Father in heaven. For where two or three are gathered together in My name, I am there in the midst of them.
> —MATTHEW 18:16, 18–20

HAVE GOD'S FAITH

Jesus is always spurring us on to the closest fellowship with Him and the Father. We please God by drawing closer to Him, and He rewards us for doing so. "But without faith it is impossible to please Him, for he who comes to God must believe that He is, and that He is a rewarder of those who diligently seek Him" (Heb. 11:6).

For this reason, God tells us in His Word to have faith in Him. When we want to encourage someone into a closer relationship with us, we will want to show them they can trust us. So God teaches us to trust Him more fully by doing amazing things for us when we're acting on the belief He will do a specific thing that He's told us He will do.

Is there anyone who can say beforehand what will be the outcome of their prayer? Yes! If God has given us a rhema—though it may be weak as a whisper or small as a mustard seed—it will happen for us if we don't doubt Him. So every time we act, trusting He will do what He's just told us He will do in this particular instance, He rewards us so we will trust Him more completely and be encouraged to draw closer.

> So Jesus answered and said to them, "Have [God's faith]. For assuredly, I say to you, whoever says to this mountain, 'Be removed and be cast into the sea,' and does not doubt in his heart, but believes that those things he says [are coming to pass], he will have whatever he says. Therefore I say to you, whatever things you ask when you pray believe that you receive them, and you will have them."
> —MARK 11:22–24

The pivotal point is this: We get faith, or believing, by hearing a rhema from God; that's the way we get God's faith, and His faith is totally devoid of doubts! When we have received that, we have the best reason to believe and there's no need to doubt.

Ministering in a word of knowledge can work in a similar

way. When God shows someone, for example, how He's healing a paralyzed man in a wheelchair, they should then have confidence to pray for that man or simply to tell him to rise up and walk. Whichever way we are led, it's because of our faith in God that we are able to act with confidence because we believe it will happen just as God has shown us, even though it may seem as outrageous as telling a mountain to move.

WHO HEARS FROM GOD

Because of God's deep love for us, He earnestly desires for us to know Him better. He goes to great lengths to reveal Himself and to directly communicate with those who diligently seek Him—hearing His voice is becoming increasingly more urgent for us every day! Here's a way to remember that the one who hears from God is willing to:

1. **Wait:** I'm taking time to hear from God because I'm making that a top priority in my life.

2. **Hear:** I'm willing to hear because I'm trusting He desires to talk with me though I don't deserve it in any way. I'm totally counting on the blood of Jesus to cover all of my unworthiness.

3. **Obey:** I value His correction as much as His encouragement. I will follow where He leads me because I believe "He loves me and He has the best plan for my life."

Chapter 7

THE END—COMPLETE IN *ONE*

The Conflict Intensifies

In the Anatomy of One, we examined the way we *serve* by being in the *flow* and doing our part in the work of ministry for the goal of being made complete in *One*—"to the measure of the stature of the fullness of Christ" (v. 13). We see that doing our part well is not only necessary preparation for being an Ultimate Survivor in this cosmic conflict, but this also is what's necessary for us to do if we wish to hasten the coming of God's kingdom.

Of course, Ultimate Survivors eagerly anticipate with bright expectations the coming of the kingdom. They see that happening at the time of the end when there will be the culmination of all of what we have pictured in the completion of The Love Connection. "And this gospel of the kingdom will be preached in all the world as a witness to all the nations, and then the end will come" (Matt. 24:14).

Therefore, we rejoice when we see today the obvious signs of the end drawing nearer, even though they may at times be deeply disturbing. They are the visible evidence of the invisible cosmic conflict that is swiftly intensifying. These unprecedented circumstances are assaulting our faith and threaten to dash our expectations. Be that as it may, the perfect forecaster of trends and future events, the Bible, tells us these troubling developments will continue to accelerate and grow even more disturbing. The good news is that it's all under the complete control of our heavenly Father; everything is according to His plan and is purely motivated by His love. Therefore, we will be witnesses to His working mightily in our midst to make His love more real and to showing Himself strong on behalf of those who trust Him.

Do these difficult times hamper or do they help God in preparing His kingdom? And what are His specific plans for strengthening our hopes in spite of how seemingly hopeless things may become? "For I know the thoughts that I think toward you, says the LORD, thoughts of peace and not of evil, to give you a future and a hope" (Jer. 29:11). Let's take another look at the conflict to see how our loving Father is working to use it in every way for our good.

The conflict entered our world when Adam opposed God, the ultimate authority. Through history this opposition, directed by the devil, has organized in various ways, like at the Tower of Babel, where they acted out their protest: "I have a better plan, and I'm looking out for me." Regardless of how frightening or all-powerful it may appear from time to time, the opposition will never overthrow God's plan for His kingdom and His Anointed One.

> Why do the nations rage, And the people plot a vain thing? The kings of the earth set themselves, And the rulers take counsel together, Against the LORD and against His [Messiah], saying, "Let us break Their bonds in pieces And cast away their cords from us." He who sits in the heavens shall laugh; The Lord shall hold them in derision. Then He shall speak to them in His wrath, And

distress them in His deep displeasure: "Yet I have [installed] My King On My holy hill of Zion."

—PSALM 2:1–6

One reason for the intensifying of conflict is that it's a result of God's orders: "He who is unjust, let him be unjust still; he who is filthy, let him be filthy still; he who is righteous, let him be righteous still; he who is holy, let him be holy still" (Rev. 22:11). Consequently, we see an extreme polarization taking place right before our eyes. Those in control of the media, politicians, our Hollywood stars, and the man on the street as well, are all being squeezed by the fear of man and its offspring, "political correctness," to join the opposition in the conflict.

Paul said, "In the last days perilous times will come" (2 Tim. 3:1), and "evil men and impostors will grow worse and worse, deceiving and being deceived" (v. 13). Yet in the midst of all that, "The righteous will hold to his way, And he who has clean hands will be stronger and stronger" (Job 17:9).

We see how God is allowing the opposition to use the powers of this world to run its program right out to the bitter end and to gain more complete control of every individual than the world has ever known. On top of that, He is also allowing great distress among nations and upon the earth so that, at times, the opposition may appear to be winning the conflict. In spite of how some will judge God's motives, the Great Arranger is allowing these perilous times as a way of arranging the state of affairs to be what actually works out in every respect for our maximum benefit and the coming of His kingdom.

> For nation will rise against nation, and kingdom against kingdom. And there will be famines,

pestilences, and earthquakes in various places. All these are the beginning of sorrows. Then they will deliver you up to tribulation and to kill you, and you will be hated by all nations for My name's sake....For then there will be great tribulation such as has not been since the beginning of the world until this time, no, nor ever shall be. And unless those days were shortened, no flesh would be saved; but for the elect's sake those days will be shortened.

—MATTHEW 24:7–9, 21–22

Let's make no mistake about it; things will become very hard to bear, for all of us. Yet God has promised us a way that guarantees our ultimate survival:

No temptation has overtaken you except such as is common to man; but God is faithful, who will not allow you to be tempted beyond what you are able, but with the temptation will also make the way of escape, that you may be able to [endure] it.

—1 CORINTHIANS 10:13

In God's wonderful compassion, He has made this way for us which is much more than just enduring hardships. It is the way to overcome the world, the flesh, and the devil in their efforts to discourage us from wanting to be all that God has planned for us to be!

Who shall separate us from the love of Christ? Shall tribulation, or distress, or persecution, or famine, or nakedness, or peril, or sword? As it is written: "For Your sake we are killed all day long; We are accounted as sheep for the slaughter." Yet in all these things we are more than [overcomers] through Him who loved us. For I am persuaded that neither death nor life, nor angels nor principalities nor powers, nor things present nor things to come, nor height nor depth, nor any other created thing, shall be able to separate us from the love of God which is in Christ Jesus our Lord.

—ROMANS 8:35–39

FOR OUR MAXIMUM BENEFIT

"Now, wait a minute! How can these things be for our benefit? Like you said, there's going to be trouble, yah, like big time trouble! Now, I can take on some persecution every now and then, but, come on! This looks like a stacked deck, stacked against us Christian guys!"

Well, as a matter of fact, it is a "stacked deck," but in the most important ways it's stacked in favor of Christians. First of all, remember we are on the winning side in the conflict. Despite the opposition's desperate efforts to break off the bonds of our Lord's authority, Jesus Christ remains always on the throne, exercising all authority in heaven and earth until all opposition to His authority is totally crushed.

> Then comes the end, when He delivers the kingdom to God the Father, when He puts an end to all rule and all authority and power. For He must reign till He has put all enemies under His feet. The last enemy that will be [abolished] is death.
>
> —1 CORINTHIANS 15:24–26

But here are some of the big benefits in the "big time trouble." That's when unbelievers are more likely to reconsider their direction in life, and be more willing to consider God's love. And for us believers, that's when things which have given us a false sense of comfort and security can be shaken and removed. Then if we allow ourself to be offended in Christ, we're allowing ourself to be distressed because we've moved out of His love. Or, on the other hand, if we don't allow our hearts to be hardened against His love, we will remain secure and unshaken. It all depends on how we answer the question He asked Peter: "Do you love Me more than these?" (John 21:15).

When we see our need for more of Him and turn to Him, He lovingly responds to our sincere calls for help and we experience more of the width, length, depth, and height of the love of Christ so that we may be filled with all the fullness of God (Eph. 3:18–19).

Let's remember when it is that we have the advantage of these benefits: It's when we're in the *flow*. So, who has the strongest desire and the best reasons to abide in God's love through thick and thin? Wouldn't it be someone who both understands and knows Him? How can anyone—once they have a grasp of God's pure motives, and have witnessed His continuing efforts to fulfill our joy—not be desirous of having more of His love?

"OK. It's good to be filled with more of God and to know His love more fully. But can't we find that without having to go through all this really painful stuff?"

If we believe nobody has "arrived" as yet and that God is still completing us right up till the day of Christ, then it's good to view the pain issue from God's perspective, like a loving father would. Let's assume you are a loving parent and you are deeply grieved for one of your children who is addicted to a drug that could destroy him. How much discomfort and pain are you willing to let him go through if you know that's the only way he can ever be freed of his addiction? Or do you rush in to help him avoid any discomfort when you know that doing so will keep him addicted to what will eventually kill him?

A good father knows much better than his children what is best for them, and our loving heavenly Father even more so. Sure, He wants us to have fullness of joy right here and now; but He's far more concerned for our being with Him and having fullness of joy forever. On top of that, He's a jealous God. He has a righteous jealousy for anything that keeps us from Him because He knows He just happens to be the very best of all that is good and satisfying for us.

In view of this, how much discomfort and pain is our loving Father willing to let us endure if He knows exactly what it will take to bring us to a place where we are able to see that our plan only makes things worse? He is always arranging things so we will have abundant opportunity to grasp this truth: "He loves me, and He has the best plan for my life."

Our oldest son's ministry is taking young people to different places around the world on short-term mission trips. Once, while in China, he was able to talk with a pastor who had been sent to a prison camp for his faith. Our son asked, "How were you able to go through that terrible kind of suffering for thirteen years?" The pastor replied, "I made adversity my friend; when it came, I welcomed it like a friend." It sounds like he has grown to understand God's ways, trust His love for him, and embrace the prunings.

> My brethren, count it all joy when you fall into various trials, knowing that the testing of your faith produces [endurance]. But let [endurance] have its [complete] work, that you may be [complete] and [entire], lacking nothing.
> —JAMES 1:2–4

During the war in Vietnam, a number of our jet pilots were shot down and imprisoned in the infamous Hanoi Hilton, where they were tortured in unimaginable ways for years. After they were released and we saw their interviews on TV and read their stories, we were impressed by the character of these truly fine men. There was a theme that popped up in several of their stories; it went something like this: "I thought I was a pretty decent person, but God knew what I needed; the experience was good for me." Or, like this, "I knew a little about God from what I had learned in Sunday school, but now, I feel I know Him."

We find it easier to count it all joy when we fall into various trials if we're seeing it as an opportunity to grow in our understanding of Christ and knowing Him more fully. It's a matter of gaining better understanding of our need for the prunings and how that can produce more of His joy in us when we choose to continue abiding in Him and His love.

In our observations of the trials that we all go through, we see that the strength and deceitfulness of the *Old* nature is truly amazing. In retrospect, we are often astonished as we have watched how desperate things had to become for a person before they were willing to lose something of their *Old* nature in order to gain more of Christ. But our Father is totally worthy of our thanksgiving and praise because He tenderly uses the utmost precision in matching the depths of our trials to the stubbornness of our *Old* nature; and He always makes a way so that we may endure it.

HIS SPIRIT IN US: HIS GLORY, OUR JOY

Understanding and knowing God more fully—that's the way we gain the joy that can carry us through the worst of times. We are thankful for our trials; they are excellent opportunities for getting to know God much better. Still, our most reliable source will always be, until Christ returns, the Bible, the written Word. Our understanding and knowing Him, however, is further aided by our being one spirit with Him so we have access to His rhema words, making it possible for us to walk and talk with Him on a daily basis. That, by itself, is truly amazing; but He makes it even better!

> If you love Me, keep My commandments. And I will pray the Father, and He will give you another [Comforter], that He may abide with you forever—the Spirit of truth, whom the world cannot receive, because it neither sees Him nor knows Him; but you know Him, for He dwells with you and will be in you. I will not leave you orphans; I will come to you. A little while longer and the world will see Me no more, but you will see Me. Because I live, you will live also. At that day you will know that I am in My Father, and you in Me, and I in you.
> —John 14:15–20

It is our heavenly Father's choice for us to have the closest kind of knowing Him and Jesus while we're in this earthly realm and He is in the heavenly realm. He's made this possible through the Holy Spirit who He's sent to abide in us. Intimate fellowship is the foremost reason for His offering the gift of the Holy Spirit to those who ask. "If you then, being evil, know how to give good gifts to your children, how much more will your heavenly Father give the Holy Spirit to those who ask Him!" (Luke 11:13)

When the Holy Spirit not only "dwells with us," but is in fact "in" us, we come into a more alive sense of God's love and presence while we are empowered with the gifts of the

Holy Spirit to be used more fully for His glory and for our joy. Ministering these gifts to others and receiving the ministry of their gifts can have a powerful impact on someone's life—like it did on mine.

The rain was falling heavily in Portland, Oregon, that day. It was loudly resounding on the roof of my little blue sports car where I was sitting after leaving the mortgage company office where I was following up on the financing of a house I had sold. A major change in my life was just around the corner; I would soon be leaving the business world and heading off in a brand-new direction. There in my car I paused to take a brief check on my perspective. Here I was, signed up to go to seminary. I wanted to help others like I had been helped—but I had never asked God if He needed any more helpers.

A thought came to me: *Why don't I ask God for a "fleece" like Gideon did? I could ask Him to stop the rain falling on my car while it was still falling all around my car. That would be a definite answer that He wanted me to be one of His helpers.* I hesitated for a few seconds, but I managed to brush the thought off and went on through the day.

Then, when I was in my apartment sitting at the table with a small candle burning, I thought of putting my hand in the flame: *If it doesn't burn me, it will be God's answering with a strong yes.* But I didn't do it. The last time I thought of asking was when I was showering: *Maybe I should ask God to make the hot water cold, and the cold water hot.* I even shed some tears, which was very rare for me in those days; but I backed away because I thought He'd probably answer, "No, We don't need you. We've got some good guys helping Us. They're better looking, smarter, and taller than you, but thanks for asking."

I was able to neatly stuff those thoughts away so they wouldn't interfere with my plans—I was still headed for seminary, and Helen and I would still be married. So, after we were married, we left for seminary in Berkeley, California.

What I encountered there was very challenging both academically and spiritually. The pressure increased, until by the end of the school year I was stressed out. Although many of the students seemed fearful of sharing real spiritual needs with one another, there was one guy, Roger, who appeared to be very much at peace with himself. He was easy for me to talk to. He told me, "You need the Holy Spirit, the power the early apostles had."

Through his encouragement, Helen and I attended a Full Gospel Businessmen's convention at the San Francisco Hilton across the bay. The program wasn't very appealing for me because I really wasn't open to the idea of being baptized in the Holy Spirit, and we left early. It was a gorgeous day out on the streets of romantic San Francisco. Helen, caught up in the mood, excitedly pleaded, "Let's go down to Fisherman's Wharf and have dinner!" I argued, "We don't have the time or the money." But I settled for a compromise; "We'll take a cable car ride to The Wharf and back—no dinner."

While we waited on a crowded street corner, a couple across the street came to my attention as people I thought I knew. I told Helen, but while she reminded me of how I seem to think I know everybody, this couple had woven their way through the crowds, and were standing right behind us. I said to this well-dressed, friendly looking guy, "I know you from somewhere." He replied with a smile, "No, Buddy, you've never seen me anywhere before in your life." Then I said I knew his wife, but again he corrected me with a smile. Noticing his FGBM pin, I quickly volunteered, "We've just come from the convention, but we're not one of them." "I knew you weren't one of them," he said. Finally, taking a big chance on his friendly manner, I asked, "What are you, some kind of mystical kook?"

"Buddy, I could tell you stories that would curl your hair." His eyes were still friendly and steady. "First off, you and your wife and my wife and I are going to get on a cable car, go down to Fisherman's Wharf, and have dinner." Struggling to appear unshaken by all of this, I said, "Well, I've got you there. We don't have any money." He showed me his wallet with a batch of big bills and said, "The Lord's given me lots of money, let's go."

Later, they told us how God had directed them to approach us while we were waiting on the street corner. It was a very enjoyable, yet very unusual four hours we spent with Dan and Sherrie, receiving answers to questions about the Holy Spirit. Before parting with them, they strongly encouraged us to come spend a weekend with them in their home near Los Angeles. I gave them my honest opinion: "That just won't happen. We don't have the time or the money."

Back at the seminary, pressure was increasing for me, but Helen was increasingly more interested in being filled with the Holy Spirit, reading books and studying the Bible. I did some investigating but I was earnestly wrestling with the fear that it might mean losing the respect of some people. I wanted to look spiritually solid—"nothing extreme or weird about me!" We met another Charismatic couple, Mel and Gingie. Mel prayed for us to receive the Holy Spirit, but "nothing happened." The next day, Helen was praying by herself when she began speaking a different language. She didn't tell me because she thought the words were something she just made up.

One morning I woke up with an irregular heartbeat. The doctor called it "extra systole." He asked if I was under some stress. I said, "Sure, I'm in seminary!" He prescribed tranquilizers. A week later I returned to the clinic because the condition had not improved. This time a psychiatrist walked into the exam room focused only on the chart in his hands. He looked up with eyes fixed directly on mine, and said rather sternly, "We'll double your tranquilizers, but that won't help. You are avoiding making a decision!" I thought, "Oh oh, looks like God's ganging up on me!" I said, "OK, I'll take care of it."

A few days later Helen came to me sweetly, but with a strength I'd never seen in her before, like a steamroller I knew I'd never be able to turn around. She said, "We have to fly down to Dan and Sherrie's to be baptized in the Holy Spirit." I protested with the usual, "Don't have the time, or the money," but to no avail. Through a series of amazing events, we wound up at Dan and Sherrie's. Shortly after arriving, we could hear Sherrie preparing dinner accompanied by her joyful announcements, "Praise God! Thank You Jesus!" In spite of this out of the ordinary setting and my irregular heartbeat, I told Helen, "Somehow, I feel right at home."

Later, they said God wanted to talk to me. I gave the OK and immediately sensed their words were from God: "My son, your way has been restless. The jagged rocks have cut your feet, the thorny bushes have torn your flesh and how I've longed to hold you to Me but you would not."

In a split second, without any outward expression, I stopped resisting Jesus. Like a boxer who refused to fight another round, I threw in the towel. Up till that moment I was only vaguely aware of my undercover resistance to Him. One obvious clue was my feeling uncomfortable whenever I heard the name of Jesus spoken with loving respect. Yet that day, with those few words, His love overwhelmed me and any of my resistance. Then came these words: "Welcome home, My son." I broke down, crying like a child. After my tears had subsided, the words resumed: "Of course, I've called you to be a minister! I ordained you while you were in your mother's womb." A heavy load of uncertainty was lifted off of me. Without their knowing, they had confirmed my mother's plea; and the "rest" that I had unknowingly prophesied, as a young boy, was now mine.

God went on to give me encouragement and guidance. He said, "I've called you to be a minister in My church, the church that I'm preparing as a bride without spot or wrinkle." He also told me to know and make the Bible an essential part of my life. After His words had ended, I remembered He had said, "I'll give you peace in your breast." I quickly checked my heart. It was back to normal and has been running well ever since.

Still later that day, I received what we had come for, the baptism in the Holy Spirit. Helen felt left out; she said to Dan and Sherri, "You've only prayed for Bob. What about me?" They said, "We think you have already received." And, of course, they were right. The next day, Pentecost Sunday, we returned to seminary and to a much more satisfying, productive last two years of my M. Div. program.

Like most people who are baptized in the Holy Spirit, we found all of the things we do in our relating to God became more alive—reading the Bible, praying, worship and praise times, and when reaching out in His name to bless others. These, of course, are marvelous changes; and we welcome the gifts of the Spirit so our ministry to others can have greater impact for good. Nevertheless, gifts of the Holy Spirit are no guarantee of maturity. Consequently, for Ultimate Survivors, the greatest benefit of the presence of the Holy Spirit comes from His major role in our being conformed to the image of Christ.

> Likewise the Spirit also helps in our weaknesses. For we do not know what we should pray for as we ought but the Spirit Himself makes intercession for us with groanings which cannot be uttered. Now He who searches the hearts knows what the mind of the Spirit is, because He makes intercession for the saints according to the will of God. And we know that all things work together for good to those who love God, to those who are the called according to His purpose. For whom He foreknew, He also predestined to be conformed to the image of His Son, that He might be the first-born among many brethren.
>
> —ROMANS 8:26–29

THE GLORY TO BE REVEALED

So the conflict's intensifying can work for our maximum benefit if we remain in the *flow*, welcoming the prunings as our friend and the Holy Spirit as our most cherished companion. In this way the intense difficulties gain for us more insight to the love that motivates our Lord and a closer, personal friendship with Him. So we are made more complete in *One*, until someday soon we'll see the fulfillment of our desires when He returns for a bride without spot or wrinkle.

At that time whatever discomfort we've been through

will seem quite trivial in comparison to what has happened *in* us. In the meantime, our fulfillment is realized through knowing that our *serving* is for the utmost purpose of seeing His kingdom come and His will being done. So let's press on as faithful *servants*, keeping our heart with all diligence to ensure at all cost that we are always open to the *flow*.

> For I consider that the sufferings of this present time are not worthy to be compared with the glory which shall be revealed in us. For the earnest expectation of the creation eagerly waits for the revealing of the sons of God.
> —Romans 8:18–19

Nature itself will rejoice to see us revealed as the sons of God when the *Old* is totally replaced with the nature of Christ. Then the works that God began in us will finally be completed; Self-serving, fear, and the other *Old* traits will be pruned away. Most noteworthy is that our deceptive heart will finally be healed—no more need to self-justify, no more fear of punishment. The work of the forever unique love of Christ will be completed in us; we will have been thoroughly forgiven—the *Old* trait of fear no longer will have a place in us!

> There is no fear in love; but [complete] love casts out fear, because fear has [punishment]. But he who fears has not been made [complete] in love. We love Him because He first loved us.
> —1 John 4:18–19

Another remarkable change will be seen at that time— we will see ourself as others see us. Although it never fooled God, our deceitful heart worked hard, distorting our perception in order to justify our denying any need for pruning. But in *serving*, we come to know the truth about our needs and the power of Christ's love so that we will be made complete in *One* and finally set free of the *Old* nature's cover-ups to see ourself clearly as we are.

> Every way of a man is right in his own eyes, But the LORD weighs the hearts.
> —PROVERBS 21:2

> For we know in part and we prophesy in part. But when that which is [complete] has come, then that which is in part will be done away....For now we see in a mirror, dimly, but then face to face. Now I know in part, but then I shall know just as I also am known.
> —1 CORINTHIANS 13:9–10, 12

A WITNESS TO ALL THE NATIONS

Looking beyond these, the consequences of our continuing in The Challenge are tremendous and far reaching. Will we settle for being just partly filled with the fullness of God, or will we press on to be completely filled with the fullness of God so that this gospel of the kingdom is preached in all the world?

"Now, wait a minute! What does my being all filled with God have anything to do with getting the gospel preached? And besides, how does my being all filled have anything to do with the end? Isn't that what we're really trying to talk about here?"

Well, those are fair questions, and I do, in fact, want to talk about "the end." Nonetheless, it's not just Ultimate Survivors who are eagerly anticipating the end; it's a lot of us who long to see Jesus, and because of these difficult times—the sooner, the better. So let's have at look some relevant scriptures.

> Then many false prophets will rise up and deceive many. And because lawlessness will abound, the love of many will grow cold. But he who endures to the end shall be saved. And this gospel of the kingdom will be preached in all the world as a witness to all the nations, and then the end will come.
>
> —Matthew 24:11–14

In this talk, Jesus was telling His disciple how the end will come. There will be a lot of deception going on, while at the same time there will be less real love around. A couple of days later, He gave the disciples, and us today, an acid test for knowing the genuine from the deception: "By this all will know that you are My disciples, if you have love for one another" (John 13:35).

When He says this gospel will be preached as a witness, "and then the end will come," a number of questions are brought to mind. First off, if this preaching is the "final preaching," is that because it's different from all other preaching, uniquely fulfilling some condition necessary for the end to come? And what is significant about this final preaching being a "witness?"

There's a classic quote of St. Francis: "Preach the gospel at all times and when necessary use words." As a matter of fact, a large percentage of people need more than just words in order to believe what they are being told. For this reason, the gospel message can be powerfully convincing when it is preached without words, if it serves as a reliable witness of God's having sent Jesus and His love.

Certainly, this can happen when the preaching is done, for example, through miraculous healings and deliverance— if they pass the acid test of love. Yet, here's when the most miraculous preaching is taking place: when people are seen sincerely loving one another, genuinely united as *One*, and laying down their souls for their friends. That's the most effective gospel preaching—convincing, verifiable proof that God sent Jesus, and He loves us like He loved Jesus.

Isn't this what Jesus prayed for, a unique—never seen before—kind of preaching? Isn't this what finally prepares His bride without any spots or wrinkles of the *Old* nature? So this is the "preaching" that will be seen in all the world— and then the end will come!

> I in them, and You in Me; that they may be made
> [complete] in one, and that the world may know
> that You have sent Me, and have loved them as You
> have loved Me.
>
> —John 17:23

We can be sure Jesus will be back. His grand hope and the hope of all creation will be realized. For now He is in heaven eagerly anticipating the answer to His prayer "until the times of restoration of all things" (Acts 3:21). But the restoring of our souls is the cutting edge of this restoration—so all of creation is waiting for us.

> For I consider that the sufferings of this present
> time are not worthy to be compared with the glory
> which shall be revealed in us. For the earnest expec-
> tation of the creation eagerly waits for the revealing
> of the sons of God. For the creation was subjected
> to futility, not willingly, but because of Him who
> subjected it in hope; because the creation itself also

will be delivered from the bondage of [decay] into
the glorious liberty of the children of God.

—ROMANS 8:18–21

So let's never abandon The Challenge, continually
abiding in His love by keeping our heart as open as possible
to the *flow* as our answer to The Question always before
us—"What am I doing with the love of Christ?"

Therefore, my beloved brethren, be steadfast,
immovable, always abounding in the work of the
Lord, knowing that your labor is not in vain in the
Lord.

—1 CORINTHIANS 15:58

ABOUT THE AUTHOR

Bob Guthrie graduated from the University of Washington with a major in finance, and received a Master of Divinity from the American Baptist Seminary of the West. He has had a variety of vocations including being a stockbroker, real estate broker, hospital chaplain, and Christian counselor.

He is motivated by a desire to see people enjoying the fullness of all that God has planned for each one of us. So, he is delighted to share the insights God has given for a better understanding of how He is lovingly involved in the challenges that come our way—that we may know and love Him more deeply. Bob is committed to carrying this message, preaching and teaching wherever possible to strengthen the Bride and hasten the coming of God's kingdom.

He and his wife, Helen, have been married for forty-seven years. They have four children and twelve grandchildren. When ministering together, they especially enjoy teaching Marriage Enrichment. They make their home in Seattle, Washington.

CONTACT THE AUTHOR

Bob may be contacted through this
website: www.ultimate-survivors.com.

www.ingramcontent.com/pod-product-compliance
Lightning Source LLC
LaVergne TN
LVHW051102080426
835508LV00019B/2024